Baba Amte
A Vision of New India

Baba Amte
A Vision of New India

Hans Staffner S.J.

www.popularprakashan.com

Popular Prakahan
Mumbai

POPULAR PRAKASHAN PVT. LTD.
301, Mahalaxmi Chambers
22, Bhulabhai Desai Road
Mumbai 400026

(3620)
ISBN-978-81-7154-674-9

Third Edition 2000
1st Reprint 2010

Printed in India
by Thomson Press (I) Ltd.
New Delhi

Published by Ramdas Bhatkal for
Popular Prakashan Pvt. Ltd.
301, Mahalaxmi Chambers
22, Bhulabhai Desai Road
Mumbai 400026

To

SADHANATAI

Whose faithful companionship made
Baba Amte's work possible,
whose thoughtful kindness
remains to me an unforgettable remembrance

Foreword

Creative humanism is the ideal which, from the very beginning, has inspired all the activities and determined all the policies of Sangamner College.

Swami Vivekananda expressed this ideal in these words:

"Education is not the amount of information that is put into your brain and runs riot there undigested all your life. We must have life building, man making, character building, and assimilation of ideas. If you have assimilated fine ideas and made them your life and character you have more education than any man who has got by heart a whole library."

Pandit Jawaharlal Nehru saw in creative humanism the ideal which should give direction to University Education: "A University Stands for humanism, for tolerance, for reason, for adventure of ideas and for search of truth. It stands for the onward march of the human race towards ever higher objectives. If the Universities discharge their duties adequately, then it is well with the Nation and the people."

Mahatma Gandhi was convinced that only creative humanism can lead to real Swaraj: "Real swaraj will dawn only when the lowest of the low in our society are uplifted."

Ideals become attractive when they are seen incarnated in great personalities: Sangamner College put the examples of great men who had lived up to the ideal of creative humanism, before its students as sources of inspiration. Thirty years ago Sangamner College pointed towards Baba Amte as a source of inspiration along with D.R. Gadgil, Karmaveer Bhaurao Patil, J.P. Naik and G.B. Sardar.

Baba Amte, at that time, was little known. Subsequent events showed that our choice was fully justified. Today Baba Amte is internationally recognized as one of the great humanists of our day. When the G.D. Birla Foundation established an international award for outstanding contribution to humanism, Baba Amte was the first awardee. When in December 1988 United Nations selected six persons to be honoured for outstanding achievements in the field of human rights Baba Amte was one of them.

Still there are comparatively few people who have a precise knowledge of all that Baba Amte did to promote creative humanism. We are glad that Father Staffner took the trouble of collecting all available literature on Baba Amte, that he spent some days at Anandwan and contacted people who could give information about Baba Amte and his work, and thus was able to publish a brief, yet authentic biography. Eighty-one year old Father Staffner is a religious man. A number of books are to his credit. His religious outlook aims at humanism. It is reflected when he speaks about the philosophy of Baba Amte's life in chapters, 'Sources of Baba Amte's Spirituality', 'Baba Amte's Spiritual Journey' and 'I am a Hindu Brahmin, but I am also a Follower of Jesus Christ.'

Baba Amte sees the main task of creative humanist in building inside human beings a sense of dignity and self-esteem by which great forces are released for building a better world. Baba Amte has great confidence in youth. His great desire is to create in the younger generation a courageous and aggressive movement for building New India.

Some people may not agree with Baba Amte's approach to some of the problems. But almost all his critics admit that he is a great humanist. Socrates in his famous speech raised one question: Why should man suffer? Baba Amte is trying to answer it firmly. In the present set-up how far will he succeed? It may be questioned but time will decide it. His value based humanitarian approach may inspire the young generation. I am hopeful about it.

To me, Baba Amte stands for -

न त्वहं कामये राज्यं न स्वर्गं न पुनर्भवम्
कामये दुःखतप्तानां प्राणिनामार्तिनाशनम्

-उपनिषद्

I aspire neither for kingdom, nor for heaven, nor for re - birth. The only yearning, I have is to relieve the aggrieved from their sorrows.

(Upanishads)

May this little biography contribute towards achieving this aim.

M.V. Kaundinya
Sangamner College, Sangamner
Maharashtra (India)

Preface

All really great movements in history start with a vision, a vision which often is called a dream. In 1910 Lenin wrote a booklet entitled: 'What Ought to Be Done?' In this booklet he outlined the action which he and his followers actually carried out when they took power in 1917. In 1910 people sneered at Lenin and said, "You are a dreamer." He replied, "I wish there were more dreamers in our party." If he had not seen it in a dream the revolution of 1917 might never have happened. That it later turned into a nightmare is a different story.

Martin Luther King started a famous speech with the words: "I had a dream..." At a time when Negroes were despised he dreamt of an America in which Negroes would enjoy equality. It is partly due to this dream that twenty years later a Negro is Mayor of New York and a Negro even can run for the Presidency.

Baba Amte has a vision of a New India, a vision of what India can be like if it is true to herself. If the youth of India is going to share this vision there is real hope that a New India will arise. If a vision has gripped the masses it becomes a power.

The life of Baba Amte poses some interesting questions. The basic question is: What moved Amte to renounce a rich inheritance and to give up a lucrative legal practice in order to devote his life to the service of leprosy patients? The other question is: Why does Baba Amte take up so many difficult and time consuming activities in spite of the fact that he is in very poor health and has more than enough to do in Anandwan?

The answer to both these questions is that from the beginning he had the vision of a New India, an India where people count more than money, power and prestige, a country where it is more important to fulfil the need of many than the greed of a few, a country in which justice, peace and joy prevail.

S. J. Hans Staffner

Acknowledgements

I am grateful to Principal M.V. Kaundinya for lending me a file containing articles and documents concerning Baba Amte and to Prof. (Miss) Grace Mathew of the Tata Institute of Social Sciences, Bombay, for having given me a cyclostyled copy of 'A Report on the Project for Documentation of Baba Amte's Work' of which she is the Project Director. Most of the information on Baba Amte was given to me by Baba Amte and Dr. Vikas Amte during my stay at Anandwan. Mrs. Shobha Phanishkar, Nagpur, and Fr. Alphons Oesch, S.J. Pune, carefully read the MS and made many helpful suggestions. I am grateful also to my superiors and to many others especially Prof. Ranganath Pathare for their encouragement and approval. Mr. K.A. Kshirsagar kindly agreed to type the Manuscript.

Contents

1

Baba Amte's Secret

What is the innermost secret of Baba Amte's life? What is the force that makes him live the way he does? What is the power that made him renounce a rich inheritance and give up a lucrative legal practice in order to become one with the outcast and suffering people?

There are many instances, of people voluntarily renouncing their wealth. The Buddha and the Buddhist monks regard unfulfilled desires the root cause of suffering and mental unrest. They renounce striving for wealth to obtain peace of mind. The Hindu sannyasis renounce wealth in order to obtain complete union with God. The members of Christian religious orders renounce the right of acquiring personal property in order to be free for God's service.

Baba Amte also must have had some good in mind which was more precious to him than the wealth which he renounced. What was it?

Murlidhar Devidas Amte was born on the 26th of December 1914 in Hinganghat, Wardha District, Maharashtra, the eldest son of a wealthy Brahmin family. His father owned 450 acres of good land in the Goraja village located near the town of Wardha and also held a post in the finance department.

From his earliest years Murlidhar was full of life. In his early years this zest for life showed itself in the tendency to enjoy himself. He liked to go out into the streets to play with other boys, he was wrestling and fighting with them and played all kinds of pranks. His father was annoyed at such unbecoming behaviour, but his mother sided with him. When he returned all dirty and dishevelled, his mother, to protect him from being punished by his father, let him in by the backdoor, prepared a bath for him, combed and brushed his hair and prepared for him the kind of sweet dishes he was fond of.

At the age of fourteen he had already a gun of his own and went out hunting boar and deer. As his home was at some distance from the school his father told the driver to take him there and collect him after class. Later he had his own Singer sports car, cushioned with panther skin.

Soon he became very fond of cinema and often attended two to three shows a day. He had a discerning mind and began to write reviews for the film magazine *The Picture-Goer*. His reviews attracted attention even in the Hollywood and led to correspondence with Greta Garbo and Norma Shearer. Norma Shearer became one of his first foreign donors when he began his work among leprosy patients and she inquired what made him do this kind of work.

When classes were over and holidays began he felt restless at home. He would take meals with his family for a day or two and then disappear, having assured his mother that he was not running away for good. He wanted to enjoy life. He travelled all over India anxious to see beautiful sights and meet interesting people. In Calcutta he was attracted by the songs and music of Rabindranath Tagore and he spent quite a time with him at Shantiniketan.

In spite of all his extra-curricular activities Baba got on well with his studies. His inclination was to study medicine. Even his initials, M.D., pointed in this direction, he says. But on this point he yielded to the wishes of his father and studied law. Soon he became a well-known and successful advocate and established a lucrative practice at Wardha. His father had three houses at his disposal in Wardha. There was also a club where he could spend his leisure hours in bridge, tennis and other pursuits befitting his station. During the week he could develop his practice and at weekends he could look after his family's big estate at Goraja, which is near Warora. With his practical bent of mind he organized co-operatives at Warora and was in various ways helpful to the people. In recognition he was elected Vice-president of the municipality. Thus he appeared to be well settled, having money and prestige in plenty.

Amte felt uneasy in a life of mere respectability. As time went on life in a rich and respectable family appeared to Amte increasingly unsatisfactory. Already in his early youth he had revolted against the way low-caste servants were treated in his house. When he wanted to play with the children of the servants he was reminded sharply that he was a high-caste Brahmin and should remember his superior status. When he ate food with them he was punished. "There is a certain callousness in families like mine," Baba says. "They put up strong barriers so as not to see the misery in the world outside and 1 rebelled against it." Amte also began to feel increasingly uneasy about the life he was leading. He says: "I, who never had planted a single seed in the estate was expected to enjoy the comfort of a beautiful farm house, while those who had toiled there all their lives had only the meanest hovels."

He was utterly dismayed when he found that on his own estate Harijans were not allowed to draw water from the village well and had to fetch it from far away. Against bitter opposition by caste people he opened the well to the Harijans.

He also felt increasingly uneasy about his law practice. He says: "I was charging fifty rupees for arguing for fifteen minutes while a labourer was getting only three-quarters of a rupee for twelve hours of toil. That was what was eating into me."

At times his legal practice forced him even to be dishonest. This bothered him still more. "A client would admit that he had committed rape, and I was expected to obtain an acquittal. And worse still, when I succeeded I was expected to attend the celebration party."

Amte is Attracted to the Poor People

From his earliest years Amte was attracted by the Gonds and other primitive people whom he met on his hunting expeditions deep in primeval forests. Their poverty, hunger and disease appalled him, but he was fascinated by their innocence and cheerfulness, their simplicity and friendliness. He also appreciated their fine artistic sense and their love and reverence for nature. He also liked to travel to remote villages to mix with the farmers and the common people in order to come to know them and to understand their problems.

Here, he felt was genuine warm life. He says: "That microscopic look at village life taught me to hear the heart-beat of reality. To me, the common man's society is a maskless society. He does not carry that thick mask which the professional people, the upper classes, wear so that they might look nice and beautiful. Very often they do not dare to say what they really think and feel."

More and more he came to dislike the life of the rich and 'respectable' people and felt drawn to the company of the poor and oppressed. He came to admire the "richness of heart of the poor people" and to despise "the poverty of heart of the rich." He repeats over and over again: "The common man, he is the uncommon man." Thus it was his very zest for a full life, his quest for being fully human and fully alive that made him inclined to become one with the poor by renouncing his wealth.

Happiness Results from Making other People Happy

There was another experience which gave direction to Amte's search for a full and fruitful life. He never forgot the experience he had when he was still a little boy. Amte relates: "We all felt happy and excited because it was Diwali. My mother had saved a lot of small coins from her shopping and gave them to me to buy crackers. Stuffed full with sweets and feeling that life was grand I ran towards the market. Then I saw a blind beggar. He sat in the hot sun by the edge of the unpaved road while gusts of wind raised clouds of dust and rubbish over him. *'Andhalalya paisa dey, Bhagwan.'* he kept on saying to the passers by. 'Give one paisa to this blind man, oh, Bhagwan.' In front of him there was a dirty rag and his begging bowl, a rusty cigarette tin. It struck me: alongside my bright happy world there was a world of misery and pain.

"I rushed across and started putting such handfuls of coins into the tin which he held out to me that it almost fell from his hand with the weight. 'I am only a beggar, young sir, don't put stones into my bowl.' 'These are not stones but coins. Count them if you wish,' I said. He sat and counted and then recounted sorting out the coins on that tattered cloth. He just could not believe it. He went on counting and feeling the coins. It made me so sad, I ran home in tears."

The awareness of so much misery in the world, the happiness in the face of the blind beggar was an experience which Amte never forgot.

Thus it began to dawn on him that the way to become fully human and fully alive was to become one with the poor and oppressed in order to lead them to a better and happier life. But he did not yet see clearly his way of accomplishing this.

Amte becomes a Sadhu

One thing was clear to him. If he got married to a girl with the normal domestic instincts the way to a life as he dreamt it would be blocked. He would be condemned to a life of respectability. Ever more ladies approached him and tried to interest him in their daughters. To stop these importunities he made it known that he had decided to become a sadhu and to take the vow of celibacy. He let his hair and finger-nails grow, smeared his body with ashes, and dressed only in a loin-cloth, sat for hours on the river sand pretending to be deeply absorbed in meditation. One day, whilst pretending to be lost in *samadhi*, a crab began pinching his thigh. "It was very painful," he told me, "but I had to pretend not noticing it. What a bluff!"

Amte discovers the Girl of His Dreams

One day something happened which opened the way to that fully human life of which he dreamt. There was a wedding in a befriended Brahmin family. He noticed that the younger sister of the bride, under some pretext or other, left the wedding party to help an old servant woman washing clothes. Normally no Brahmin girl would ever think of doing such a thing. It struck him like a flash: here was a kindred spirit. This was the kind of girl in whose company he could realize his ideal. He felt already as if he were married to her.

The father of the girl was a well-known pandit. Her family, the Ghuleshastris, had been Sanskrit scholars for several generations. The girl was called Indu, though her real name was Sadhana. A few days later Amte saw Indu's mother, and announced that he was about to give up his vow of celibacy. When she asked why, he replied that he had found a bridegroom for Indu. "But what has that got to do with your vow?" "Because I am the candidate," Amte announced.

The poor woman received the shock of her life: The preliminaries for an Indian marriage are usually more indirect and circumspect. Besides Amte's past, his notoriety and now his manner of proposal, all were radically wrong.

Ultimately Indu's mother gave her consent and the day of the marriage was fixed. Three weeks before the celebrations were due to begin, when the bridegroom was staying at the Ghuleshastri's house, two thieves broke in during the night. One of them went off to ransack the house while the other stood with his dagger poised over Baba, thinking he was asleep. Suddenly Baba got him a leg scissor lock, and they rolled over the bed and floor. His friend came running back but Baba managed to hit him in the testicles. Both of them set on Baba with their knives and they stabbed him repeatedly. One would have stabbed him even around the neck, had Baba not caught the blade.

The thieves eventually ran away. With sixteen wounds on his body, Amte was rushed to the Mayo Hospital at Nagpur, where at first he was not expected to survive more than a few hours. But on account of his strong constitution he recovered.

When in December 1946 Amte stepped on to the marriage altar he was swathed in bandages.

At the wedding itself he resolved to renounce his property and to give up his legal practice.

As a first attempt to become one with the poor people Baba Amte and Sadhanatai set up a *shram-ashram* (work camp) near Warora. They set up an open house and anyone was free to join them. Before long more than twenty people had joined them. One poor Brahmin family who knew something about agriculture, one shoemaker, one umbrella repairer and a few harijans; one of them brought three wives along, who were constantly quarrelling, dirty and full of lice. R.K. Patil, a local politician, loaned them seven acres of scrub land on the outskirts of Warora. Living in fraternal harmony they cultivated the land in common, cooking and eating in one kitchen, pooling their incomes. To enable them to make a start by buying implements, seed, manure and the like, Amte spent the money he had saved from his legal practice.

In October 1947 Amte's first son Vikas was born. The baby was born in the local maternity home. Contrary to the usual practice, the delivery occurred without any help coming from Indu's family. Indu says, without any rancour, that she could not think of going to her mother's house where, owing to the people with whom they mixed, she and her husband would be outcasts themselves. Nor could she expect her mother to come to Warora to live in their house whose occupants included harijans. Nobody came to see their son Vikas.

Amte continued to be involved in various organizations. He was not only Vice-chairman of the Warora Municipality but also Chairman of the scavengers' union. When the scavengers went on strike demanding better conditions and wages he was willing to fight their case. When he talked with them they asked, "Will you be able to do the dirty work we are doing daily? When you carry the night soil on a rainy day you will know what our work is like!

Amte accepted the challenge and did the work of a scavenger not just for a day, but for the next nine months.

An Experience that Changed His Life

Returning home on a rainy evening he saw something lying on the road which looked like a bundle of rags. Coming closer he found that it was a leprosy patient in the last stage of illness, a living corpse, two holes gaped where the nose should have been, no fingers, the body was naked and maggots crawled all over. Overcome by fright Amte ran away. He was afraid of infection. He thought of his wife and children to whom he might communicate the infection, therefore he ran away.

Soon he began to loathe himself. What a coward he was: There was a dying man, lonely and forsaken, lying out there in the rain, naked, and in great pain and he had run away, because he was afraid. He forced himself to return, gave food to the sick man, put up a bamboo shed to protect him against the rain and cared for him till he died. That man was Tulshiram.

Baba never could forget that sight. He recalls, "The image of that dying leprosy patient was burning me like a branding iron and would not give me a moment's rest. From that moment on I was out to conquer fear." It had become clear to Amte that without conquering fear he could not remain true to what was best in him; he could not remain true to God. "Where there is fear, there is no love. Where there is no love there is no God."

For six months he remained restless. For hours he discussed with his wife whether they should devote their life to the service of leprosy patients. At that time leprosy was still thought to be highly infectious. They carefully considered the risk they were taking.

His wife assured him, "You must follow the dictate of your heart. I shall find my happiness in following you." Amte says, "Finally we decided to banish fear and to build a friendship of pain with our suffering brothers and sisters. We entrusted ourselves to the care of God."

What is Baba Amte's Secret?

When we ask what is the basic drive which led Baba Amte to renounce his wealth and to devote his life to the service of leprosy patients we find it is the drive to be fully human and fully alive; it is the determination to find a way of life which leads to genuine joy and to a true sense of fulfilment. He has achieved this aim. He has found true joy in Anandwan, the Jungle of Joy.

When on March 2, 1990 he left Anandwan to settle down on the bank of the river Narmada he said: "The time has come to leave Anandwan, the place where I entered into the world of joy, the place that symbolises the very meaning of my existence." (*The Hitvada,* March 4, 1990)

He achieved his aim by practising the *sadhana,* the yoga, recommended by the main stream of India's ancient spiritual *culture.* It is the *sadhana* expressed in the prayer:

From the unreal lead me to the real.
From darkness lead me to the light.
From death lead me to immortality.

(Brihad Aranyaka Upanishad, 1:3:28)

It is the *sadhana* that taught him to distinguish between illusion and reality, it is the yoga that led him to organise his life around his true self.

Amte's quest for a genuine life and for lasting joy proceeded in two stages: in the first stage he realised that genuine, warm life is found in the company of the common people rather than in the society of the rich and respectable people. This insight led him to give up his wealth and position in order to become one with common people in a *shram-ashram*.

The second step was to build a friendship of pain with leprosy patients. It was again the quest for a full life by remaining true to himself that led him to take this second step.

When he had run away in fright from Tulshiram, the dying leprosy patient, he became disgusted with himself. He was known to be fearless, and he was proud of it and now, out of fear, he had left a dying man, exposed to rain in a gutter, without helping him. He said: "I have never been frightened of anything. Because I fought British tommies to save honour of an Indian lady Gandhiji called me *abhay sadhak*, a fearless seeker of truth. When the sweepers in Warora challenged me to clean gutters, I did so. But that same person who fought goondas and British bandits quivered in fright when he saw the living corpse of Tulshiram, no fingers, no clothes with maggots all over."

The incident to which Amte refers occurred as follows:

Amte was travelling in a train and a group of British tommies happened to be his fellow travellers. In the same compartment there was a newly married couple, a young tahsildar and his wife. The wife, a shy woman, became the focus of attention of the soldiers who started teasing her with verbal comments some of which were boorish and vulgar. The husband appeared to be too frightened to defend his wife. Amte chivalrously rose to the occasion by raising a strong protest against the teasing, but his protests were of no avail. The situation became worse when the verbal argument turned into a physical tussle between Amte and the soldiers. Though Amte's early experience as a wrestler stood him in good stead, he could not prevail against the collective muscular strength of the group for long. He was beaten badly and thrown out of the compartment. But he did not give up his fight. He did not allow the train to leave the platform till he got the assurance that proper action would be taken against the soldiers from the commandant of the regiment who had to be called to the spot to settle the matter. (*A Report* :p 9-10).

This yielding to fear and his failing to help a human being who was in extreme need shattered Baba Amte's self-image. Looking into himself he no longer saw a fearless person, but a coward. He confesses: "I am upset, I am very much disappointed when I see within myself a wrong image of myself " (*Ujjwal Udyasathi,* p.24). It was clear to him, if he could not banish this fear, he could not have any self-respect any more. His life would be the life of a defeated person. He would be like a bird whose wings have been broken. He had rightly said: "A man can live without fingers, but he cannot live without self-respect." He would have lost that self-image which makes life worth living. The real reason why he took up leprosy work was to overcome that fear: "That is why I took up leprosy work. Not to help anyone, but to overcome that fear in my life. That it worked out good for others was a by-product. But the fact is : I did it to overcome fear" (*The Illustrated Weekly of India,* May 20, 1984, p. 15).

Amte gave up his wealth, not in a spirit of religious renunciation, but because he saw in his wealth a hindrance to his quest for being truly human and fully alive, and he did take up leprosy work, not to help others, but because he was resolved to remain true to himself. In doing this he was guided by India's ancient spiritual tradition which taught him a fine sense for discerning true human values and which had made him understand that at times true heroism is required to remain true to ourselves. Amte can be regarded as a modern *sadhak* or yogin in the best sense of the term..

2

Amte's Miracle: Anandwan

Once the major decision had been taken Amte acted fast. he read all the books about leprosy which he could find and went to work in the Warora leprosy clinic. This clinic was run by a government doctor who took little interest in the patients. Only two or three patients attended on a day. Soon Amte opened his own leprosy clinic. Now people turned up in hundreds and Amte was busy from eight in the morning till late in the evening diagnosing, giving injections, cleaning out ulcers with a knife and dressing wounds. The government called him a quack, but there was no one else around.

To gain further experience Amte started commuting twice a week to a leprosarium at Sattapur which was run by a devoted Gandhian, Manohar Divam. Amte learned fast. After a few months Divam realized that Amte now needed more technical, medical knowledge and advised him to attend a specialized course at the Calcutta School of Tropical Medicine.

Since he had not done any preparatory medical studies Amte found it difficult to get admission. It is said that Pandit Jawaharlal Nehru's personal intervention was required. Finally, in 1949 he was admitted. One day he heard a lecturer say that one of the greatest obstacles to the progress in curing leprosy was that they could not grow germs in the usual testing animals. Perhaps, he added with a smile, that human beings would be the best laboratory specimens.

It took Amte two days to think it over. Then he came forward and said that he was prepared to be a human guinea pig. "The halo of Fr. Damian was before me," he said, "and I knew that Sadhana would nurse me." First he was injected with dead bacilli taken from positive cases of leprosy, and when that was ineffective, with the live bacillus itself. Even that failed to take hold and the experiment had to be abandoned.

In spite of having no preparatory medical training Amte stood first in a course made up of medical students and qualified doctors.

By the time Amte arrived back at Warora the treatment of leprosy had been revolutionised by the discovery and availability of the Sulphone drug, diamino-diphenyl-sulphone, known as DDS or dapsone. Provided the sickness was discovered early enough and tablets were taken every week it effected a cure in well over ninety-five per cent of the cases and brought relief to millions. Having this wonderful drug at hand Amte began treating leprosy cases not only at Warora but also in sixty surrounding villages. Soon he had set up eleven weekly clinics, within a radius of about 50 km. from Warora, with a total of about 4000 patients.

Curing the Whole Person

Amte was fully aware that merely arresting the progress of the disease was not enough. Leprosy not only harms the body, but inflicts deep wounds on the mind. It destroys the personality. Traditionally leprosy patients are excluded from society and even from their own family. With their face disfigured, crippled in hands and feet, they are shunned by all. Even if their disease is arrested and they are no longer infectious, it makes little difference. Who knows who is infectious and who is not. They remain condemned to sit on the road and beg for alms. Thus their self-respect is destroyed, the joy of loving companionship has gone out of their lives. This hurts more than losing one's fingers and toes. Amte rightly says: "A man can live without fingers, but he cannot live without self-respect."

What is required is a cure of the whole person, these disfigured and despised people have to be rebuilt into respected and self-respecting people within a happy and cheerful community.

How could such a Miracle be Performed?

First of all these people had to be made self-supporting. Amte's basic insight is: Charity destroys, work builds up a person. The most obvious way of becoming self-supporting is to run a farm; to grow grain and vegetables both for one's own consumption and for sale. With the help of friends Amte founded the 'Warora Maharogi Seva Samity'. This society was registered in 1951 and in the same year it obtained from government a grant of 50 acres of scrub land on which they could set up the kind of 'farm cum leprosarium' which Amte had in mind.

A Heroic Start

The land which he had received was barren, rock-ridden wasteland 5. km. from Warora. It was covered with scrubs and trees and richly populated with cobras and scorpions. There was no water anywhere in the vicinity. The nearest well was 2 km. away. Amte says: "I looked at it with profound emotion and perhaps a tinge of dismay. It was more than just a disused quarry, it was like looking into my own future, a new volume of my life. Perhaps it was symptomatic that there was nothing but a tangle of boulders, roots and creepers. Outcast land for outcast men. This was our lot from now on, I thought."

Becoming One with the Suffering People

One thing was clear to Amte: If he wanted to restore the awareness of their human dignity in his leprosy patients he could not work for them, he had to work with them. They had to be treated as responsible subjects who know and act, not as objects who are known and acted upon.

He selected six highly positive male patients, two old and four young, and he asked them whether they were willing to try to turn this deserted land into a farm that could support them. All depended on the possibility of finding water, and that was by no means assured.

"Friends," he told them, "we must dig for water. We want to turn this waste-land into green fields. But we are not going to beg for help; as you know to your own cost, beggars receive more injury than gifts. Charity destroys, but work builds. Are you going to join me?"

For a moment the deformed and ugly, the lame and ailing kept quiet, visualizing the enormity of the task ahead.

Even if they found water, to clear the jungle meant years of back-breaking work; moving the boulders, carrying the stones away, uprooting trees and shrubs. Such work would be almost impossible for able - bodied men but most of these men suffered from crippling deformities in hands and feet. And they were desperately poor. Their total assets were one lame cow and fourteen rupees in hand. How could they attempt this?

But such was the respect in which they held Amte that with one accord they shouted, "When can we start?" At that moment Anandwan, the forest of joy, was born.

A Hard Beginning

The first requirement was to build two shelters, thatched roofs on bamboo poles with no walls, which left them defenceless against wild animals at night. The four dogs they had brought with them for their protection were carried off, one by one, by panthers.

They started digging a well. They possessed four shovels, two hoes, three pick axes, and two crow-bars. It was not so much a question of digging as cutting and breaking through the rock.

Amte described vividly the sinking of the well.

"After about six weeks, when we were about 34 feet down, the rock was becoming a little moist. It was in May; the temperature ran to 47 degrees Celsuis in the shade. Inside the hole it was fearfully hot. Then a bee followed by a butterfly came to the moisture. Two days later when we arrived in the morning we found a frog happily sitting in a puddle of water between the stones. Three days later water came through in abundance. We worshipped the water with white flowers and milk. Then for the rest of the day we sat by our well just staring delighted at the water. Now we had reason to look hopefully into the future."

Life in these early days was very hard. They were so short of money. They had no milk, no curds, and vegetables only once a week. Amte was so desperate that he went to a rich man's house to ask for help. The servants said the man was not at home, though Amte knew he was in. He left almost in tears and decided he would never again ask for money. Somehow they survived. The lonely lame cow they had started with was replaced in time by two others from the local Gorakstan, the home for old cows. After a year they were given a pair of bullocks. Soon they could grow not only vegetables but also prepared fields for growing millets bajri and jowar.

Steady Growth

Word about Anandwan spread quickly. Now this was a place where leprosy victims enjoyed self-respect and worked for themselves. In 1954 there were about sixty patients and they had dug six wells. Some of the fifty acres had been cleared of jungle and large crops of grain and vegetables could be harvested.

Loading his bullock cart with potatoes, beetroot, brinjals and cauliflower Amte went to the market at Warora and spread out his tempting produce. Admiring glances were cast at the quality. His prices were reasonable, but buyers were scarce. "How can we eat these vegetables?" they said "Do you want us to catch leprosy?"

Amte himself, since he had made himself one with the leprosy patients, was regarded as a leper. No one ever came to visit him. No one even dared to invite him for tea. His two boys had no one to play with. "I am more isolated than my patients are," he said. Yet he was happy in the company of his patients. By this time Amte had become Baba Amte, and Sadhana had become Sadhanatai, tai means sister.

Unexpected Help

With the influx of so many new patients - many in urgent need of treatment - better accommodation and treatment facilities became a necessity. Help came from an unexpected quarter. Fifty young workers of the 'Service Civil International', belonging to 36 different countries, were engaged in building work at Gandhi's Ashram at Sevagram, which is 100 km. from Warora. When they heard of Amte's need for new buildings they came to Anandwan and offered their services. Within three months they had built a clinic and two spacious hospital wards.

Amte and his wife had recommended themselves to God's providence. Their faith was rewarded by this unexpected intervention. Amte often repeated: "Wherever God has pointed the way with his finger, he also cleared the way with His mighty palm." Trusting in divine providence Amte resolved never to turn away any homeless person that asked for shelter. He would never think of his budget or whether there was food to spare but in good faith take in everyone who asked for help.

The coming of the volunteers also effected a change of heart in the people of Warora who, till then, had shunned Anandwan. Observing how these foreigners helped they also felt like doing something and donated food for the volunteers. Seeing that these Europeans were not afraid of infection by staying at Anandwan, some people from Warora also began visiting the place. Differently at first, they looked round and found with some surprise that Anandwan was very much like any other farm except that it was better run. From then on Amte had little difficulty in selling vegetables in Warora.

Connection with Swiss Aid

Pierre Oppliger, who had been the leader of these volunteers, later became the representative in India of Swiss Aid, an organization giving help to developing countries. This led to a fruitful cooperation between Anandwan and Swiss Aid.

Anandwan had become self-supporting as far as the daily running was concerned. But outside help was required for constructing new buildings and workshops for the quickly increasing number of residents. Once a year Swiss Aid sent an appeal to the French speaking cantons of Switzerland. Many people gave up a meal and sent the savings through Swiss Aid to Amte. Under Schnellmann this aid continued. In recent years, however, the policy of Swiss Aid changed. They are interested now in different kinds of projects.

Leprosy Patients Become Benefactors

Baba Amte not only aimed at rebuilding the personality of single patients but at changing the attitude of the society towards people afflicted with leprosy. It seemed to him that the most effective way of doing this was by changing leprosy patients from beggars into benefactors of healthy people. When leprosy patients will be at the giving end as benefactors instead of always being at the receiving end as beggars their position in society is bound to be changed.

Already in 1962 when China had invaded India the patients at Anandwan staged a play which raised Rs. 2000/- for the National Defence Fund. Now Baba Amte had a bigger plan: The patients at Anandwan, out of their own income would start two University Colleges for the people of Warora. Warora, being an out-of-the way place had no University College. Starting a college would meet a real need of the people and would fulfil the aspiration of some of the better gifted rural boys and girls who longed for higher education. Students attending classes within Anandwan were bound to lose the fear of coming close to leprosy patients. The patients not only erected the buildings but made all the furniture and did all the fittings themselves. The cost, Rs. 2,50,000 was raised by the sale of the produce from a land which once had been regarded as useless. As the agriculture at Anandwan, being very well conducted, showed by that time a yearly surplus of nearly one lakh, such an undertaking had become feasible. In July 1964 the Anand Niketan College of Arts, Science and Commerce was ready. It is affiliated to the Nagpur University. In 1965 the Anand-Niketan College of Agriculture also started working. It is affiliated to the Punjabrao Krishi Vidyapeeth. Agricultural University of Akola. Today they are well run colleges with more than 2000 students.

Besides the two Colleges there is at Anandwan a primary school, a school for blind children and a school for deaf-mutes. They attend the High School at Warora. The children are brought there daily by bus.

One day an infant girl, abandoned by her mother, was found at Warora railway station and was brought to Anandwan. When it became known that Amte does not refuse shelter to anyone in need, other orphan children followed. There were also a number of children from leprosy patients who could not remain with their parents for fear of infection. Thus the need for an orphanage arose. Baba Amte appealed to the school children of Maharashtra for help in starting this orphanage. The school children of Maharashtra enthusiastically responded and collected Rs. 3,50,000. This home, called Gokul, is brightened today by the faces of 50 happy children.

Baba Amte not only wants his patients to become self-supporting, he wants them to be cultural people. He stimulates their growth in aesthetic appreciation and creativity. He wants them to enjoy beauty and to create beauty. In 1961 he started in Anandwan a three-day programme called Mitra Melawa (a get-together of friends) *Mitra Melawa* is a cultural festival to which the public are invited; it is a feast of music, dance and drama. Artists are invited from outside and the inmates also stage dramas. It was on such an occasion that P.L. Deshpande, the renowned Marathi writer, got interested in Amte's work. When he saw leprosy patients performing a drama for outsiders he mused: "Usually people avoid seeing leprosy patients. Here Baba is putting them on the stage for all to see." He found this so captivating that he gave a large donation for the construction of an auditorium with a stage and also an open air stage for the staging of cultural programmes. Baba wants the Anandwan people to have a taste of the best in music and drama and he got some famous artists like Kumar Gandharva, Shriram Lagoo and Ravi Shankar to perform for them.

Sandhi Niketan (Home of Opportunities)

Anandwan soon became a flourising institution. Patients flocked to it from all over India, e.g., from West Bengal, Andhra Pradesh, Tamil Nadu. The state government gave to Amte another 200 acres. In 1954 Amte bought six cows; the following year a proper dairy was started with 25 heads of cattle.

Whereas to this point they had concentrated nearly exclusively on agriculture, the time had come to branch out into tailoring, weaving, printing, metal work, leather work and other trades.

In 1968 Baba Amte acquired a new friend in the person of Count Arthur Tarnowski. Tarnowski, a Pole by birth, who emigrated to England, suffered from polio and is confined to a wheel chair. This did not prevent him from travelling all over the world to see for himself the service provided for the physically disabled. In India. Having heard of Anandwan he went there and explained to Amte his idea of putting up a technical wing in which the leprosy patients and other handicapped people could learn a trade. Amte said, "I shall try."

When, in 1970 Count Tarnowski travelled all the way from England to Anandwan to find out whether Amte had forgotten his suggestion, Amte told him, "You have come a long way to talk to me, but I have a surprise for you : I have worked out most of the details already." Tarnowski was given a big sheet of paper and to his amazement he saw that it was a complete plan with rooms for 25 trainees, craft training halls, physiotherapy gymnasium, kitchen, storerooms, quarters for staff, bathrooms, everything. "Baba, from where did you get an architect to do all these drawings?" "Architect? An architect here? We do the drawings ourselves." Tarnowski looked at the plan with amazement. He marvelled at the precision and neatness with which each dimension had been inscribed.

"But how much will this cost?" Tarnowski asked with some apprehension since he had promised to find the money. "Well, I haven't quite finished my calculations". Amte replied "But I should think about £9,500/- for the construction. Another £2000/- for equipment and the running cost of the first three years; and another £14,000 to bring water to the experimental training farm." "You realize that I have no money yet" said Count Tarnowski, "It is a great deal to raise!" "I have never had money", said Amte, "but that had never stopped me." "I agree with you perfectly", was Tarnowski's reply. "All that I can offer now are the royalties for my book. This should help us to get started at least." Amte paused and gave him a searching look; "If you give the royalties from your book, I shall give the land."

The next day Tarnowski went out on his wheelchair to watch the building work in progress, work done by leprosy patients with hands and feet in various degrees deformed. Today hundreds of patients find work in Sandhi-Niketan. More than 40 trades are taught and practised and all branches insist on quality.

Dr. Vikas and his Wife Dr. Bharati Come to Help Baba Amte

Baba Amte had always been anxious to have a fully trained doctor to help him in the medical work. But the fear of infection proved to be a great obstacle. When he called a doctor in the event of some particular illness the doctor carefully washed not only himself but also his cycle on leaving Anandwan.

Baba's son Vikas would have liked to become an engineer, but seeing the need of a doctor at Anandwan he studied medicine, this wife Bharati, is also a fully trained doctor. Both share Baba Amte's complete dedication to the uplift of leprosy patients. His inclination to engineering is of great help to Dr. Vikas especially in running Sandhi Niketan. He says, "I have to cure both men and machines." Dr. Vikas joined Anandwan in 1974 and for all practical purposes has taken over the management of the institution. He carried a heavy load as manager of people and resources, project planner, public relations officer and fund raiser. He faithfully follows the spirit in which his father has started the institution. Baba, on the other hand, has full confidence in Dr. Vikas and encourages him to follow his own independent judgement and initiative.

Dr. Vikas gets many invitations from all over the world to attend high level meetings of development workers. He attended a few such meetings, but finds them rather a waste of time. He says, "There are too many paper pregnancies."

Like Baba, so also Dr. Vikas, insists on following a life - style which is not much different from that of the patients. To a man of his abilities highly paid jobs would be open for the asking. In Anandwan he lives on a salary of Rs 500/- a month. I was struck when I asked him to send me some photos for an article I intended to write, he replied, "No photos are available here, nor have we a camera."

Some Special Features of the Life at Anandwan

A special feature of the life at Anandwan is the stress on quality. Not only is the place kept perfectly clean, full of flowers, the houses all freshly painted in bright, cheerful colours. There is the greatest care in water management, all the waste water is carefully collected in a big pond. In flower shows Anandwan's roses were sure to get the first prize and so did Anandwan's cows and buffaloes in animal exhibitions. Anandwan keeps abreast of the latest scientific research, in its endeavour to improve the soil and in producing the best possible seed. High yielding seeds produced by Anandwan are bought in bulk by the National Seeds Corporation. This explains why the crop yields per acre are higher at Anandwan than in the neighbouring regions. The following table of crop yields in quintals per acre may be of interest.

Crop	Anandwan	Chandrapur District	Maharashtra
Rice	9.0	4.0	5.3
Wheat	10.0	2.0	3.1
Hybrid Jowar	15.0	1.8	2.8

(Note: These and the following tables are taken from A Report of Baba Amte's Work made by Tata Institute of Social Sciences, Bombay, 1988)

By taking great care to improve the soil, by using natural manure and the best seed Anandwan managed to become financially independent. Over the years agriculture yielded a considerable surplus.

(In Rupees)

Year	Income	Expenditure	Surplus
1951-52	494-00	164-00	330-00
1953-54	2,201-00	1,310-00	891-00
1958-59	21,258-00	5,173-00	16,085-00
1965-66	38,800-00	10,198-00	2,98,602-00
1974-75	2,82,105-00	1,68,335-00	1,13,770-00
1983-84	14,00,149-00	7,64,325-00	6,35,824-00
1984-85	17,14,932-00	9,60,120-00	7,54,812-00
1985-86	19,80,623-00	11,04,233-00 8,	76,390-00

These figures do not really give an exact picture, because only cash income and expenditure appear to be considered, grain used for home consumption does not seem to have been included.

In 1964 it was still possible to put enough money aside to build three colleges for the people of Warora, because there were only 660 inmates in Anandwan.

In 1984 there were 1,800 inhabitants. When asked what would happen if financial support from outside would dry up, Amte could reply, "Capital intensive projects like laying water pipelines, constructing buildings and major repairs would have to be deferred, but the normal activities would continue unimpaired." Today (1990), when the number of inhabitants has risen to 2,500 Anandwan has to confess that they cannot continue without outside help. Much of the cash surplus has to be used to buy additional grain and pulses.

FOOD BALANCE (1985-86)

Foodgrains	Annual consumption	Annual Deficit	Surplus
Wheat	2250	490	-1760
Jowar	500	355	-145
Rice	1500	2010	510
Pulses	400	70	-330

Yet the greatest danger threatening Anandwan results from indications that there may be big coal deposits in that region. In February 1989 already Government gave them notice not to start any new building etc. Government will argue that they can do their work also elsewhere. Well, but what about the tremendous efforts which they have made for the last forty years to improve the land?

How People Are Cared for at Anandwan

Anandwan provides for each inhabitant food, clothes and shelter. Stated in prices as they were in 1985 this roughly means: for food Rs. 910/-, clothing Rs. 200/- shelter Rs. 190/- in all Rs. 1,300/-. In addition people get an allowance or incentive payment for work done. The maximum payment at present is Rs. 500/- a month. Even Baba Amte or Dr. Vikas, inspite of the tremendous work load which they carry, do not draw more than that. The result is that salaries amount to just one per cent of the total expenditure of about a million rupees.

Financial Control

About the financial control at Anandwan a Unicef Report, New Delhi, (December 1983), has the following to say: "The system of management at Anandwan incorporates an interesting labour saving and as good a computerised financial accounting and control. For instance, each activity at Anandwan like growing vegetables, maintaining a dairy, raising of cotton or jowar crops or running a grocery store, is deemed a distinct unit expected to support itself and gain a surplus, to be ploughed back for further development in directions of priority. Everyday each unit meets its expenses by bank withdrawals specific to each item. Similarly, each component of income is credited to the bank account against self-explanatory entries in the passbook. No other accounts are needed. And the passbook presents an up-to-date picture of the financial status with sufficient details for managerial appraisal and audit."

Self-Management

A non-bureaucratic, self-governing culture pervades Anandwan. One proof of this vital management attribute is the fact that Anandwan functions smoothly when Baba is away for fairly long periods for treatment in London or in Bombay, or on tour to remote tribal belts or the 'Bharat-jodo' Yatras.

Anandwan has little use for degree-holders in management. Everything runs smoothly, supervised not by degree-holders but by people crippled in hand and feet, who have learned everything by experience, by self-made technicians, technologists, draughtsmen and scientific farmers. Only an awakening of self-awareness can explain the marvels typical of the place : structures, strong and functional without architects, engineers and contractors; weavers without fingers, leprosy patients successfully insisting on being licensed to drive heavy duty trucks; a man who cannot walk managing the industrial training centre moving on a tricycle fabricated at Anandwan; a person without previous experience running a printing press with competence, a one-handed cashier who makes up for slight slowness by unusual thoroughness; a master tailor who cannot use his hands freely training tailors from neighbouring villages, besides catering at low cost to the needs of people in and outside Anandwan.

The Secret of Anandwan's Success

The real mystery is the joy, the contentment, the mutual love and consideration that pervades the institution. Baba Amte rightly says: "Joy is more infectious than leprosy." After having stayed for several days at Anandwan I became convinced that the secret of its success lies in Baba having made himself one with the inhabitants and that Sadhanatai, Dr. Vikas and Dr. Bharati share the same spirit. The spirit of any community, to a large extent, is created by the one who is in charge. The response of the community largely depends on his approach. It follows the rule of an echo. If you should say "I love you" the echo is "I love you." If you shout "I don't care for you" the answer is "We do not care for you either."

Baba not only has made himself one with the patients but shows to each of them the most tender affection and care. There are some cottages with old and infirm people. Baba makes it a point to visit them every day and to talk to each of them, because he knows what personal contact means to these people. The whole institution is full of roses and flowers, but Baba is very careful to raise roses without thorns near the cottage of blind children. Kindness, cheerfulness and tenderness, by a kind of osmosis, seem to spread over the whole institution. Anandwan is a complete village, fully self-supporting. They produce everything they need except sugar, salt and petrol; but it is a village without police or any law-enforcing agency, a self-governing culture pervades Anandwan.

3

Amte's Vision of a New India

In 1930 when Gandhiji left his ashram at Sabarmati to start the Salt March, Amte was only 16 years old, too young to take an active part. In 1936 Amte took a law degree and when the Quit India movement started he was in a position to take part in the movement. He organized lawyers to take up the defence of the jailed leaders and was thrown into prison for his efforts.

The way people were united during the independence movement, the courage with which they faced the might of the British Empire remained an inspiring remembrance to Amte.

India had gained political independence. But was this really the end of the liberation movement? There is still so much misery in India. Many people have not enough food to eat, nor clothes to put on, nor a place to stay. There is so much unemployment and the slums are growing.

Mahatma Gandhi had said: "Real swaraj will dawn only when the lowest of the low in our society will be lifted up." This is also Baba Amte's conception of *Purna Swaraj* (Complete Independence).

Baba Amte's success in building Anandwan had a two-fold impact on his mind. It increased his desire to lead India's suffering millions to a resolute effort at self-development and it strengthened his conviction that this could be done by rousing the impoverished masses to a creative awareness. He had started his work in Anandwan under the most difficult conditions; he started with outcast people on outcast land. In spite of this he built up a community in which joy and contentment reign, a community which could become benefactors to the healthy people of their surroundings, a community which can send money home to their poor relatives.

He, therefore, asks: "If we could build up a happy community under the most difficult circumstance, why cannot healthy people do the same under much more favourable circumstances? Why can the youth of India not do the same?

"If an outcast man on outcast land can lead a new life, can produce not only sufficient food for himself, but help the healthy society by capital formation, can rejuvenate, why can the healthy people with healthy hands not do the same thing on good land? This is my heartache!"

Anandwan also helped Baba Amte to get a clearer idea of what the New India, the India of his dreams could be like. Amte is not fond of paper work. He does not expound big theories. He is a creative artist. He says: "My work is my pulpit. God has given me one mouth, but two hands. I am preaching with my hands." In order to tell people what the India of his dreams is like, Baba Amte constructed of a model of it on a small scale: Anandwan is the model.

India shaped on the model of Anandwan will be a country where people count, where man will be the centre, not power and wealth; where things will be arranged so as to supply everybody's needs rather than a few people's greed. A country where the rich and powerful will have no privileges and the weak and suffering will be cared for, a country where people will regard one another as brothers and sisters and share each other's joys and sorrows.

In particular, the New India will have the following characteristics:

It will be a Country in which Joy and Contentment Reign

Anyone who stays at Anandwan even for a short time is struck by the joy and contentment which pervade the place. Amte rightly says, "Joy is more infectious than disease."

Joy and contentment are based on creative work. Amte's basic principle is: 'Charity destroys, work builds up'. From the beginning he told his leprosy patients: "We are not going to beg for help. You know at your own cost that beggars receive more injuries than gifts." Amte knows that people can live without fingers, but cannot live without self-respect. People who have lost seven fingers he asks: "But what are you doing with the other three?"

The only way of restoring self-respect is to make people self-supporting. He made his leprosy patients not only self-supporting, but enabled them to become benefactors of the healthy people in their surroundings. Creative work is the basis of their self-respect.

The New India will be a country where "the mind is without fear and the head is held high", a country where people are proud of being self-supporting by hard work. Amte says: "My basic principle is that charity destroys and only work builds, and that is how the nation should be run. But we are building up a nation of welfare addicts.

"From the most ancient times it has been recognized that any orderly community or nation must have two pillars: Mutual recognition of rights and mutual cooperation for the common good. The New India will pay special attention to the strengthening of these two pillars."

Mutual Recognition of Rights

Every human being has a tendency to develop his abilities by creative work. Every human being has right to learn and to grow and this right must be respected. In many countries only the children of the elite have an opportunity to learn and to develop their talents. The children of the poor are deprived of such opportunities and, therefore, they remain backward. In building up Anandwan and Himalaya, Baba Amte not only respected this right to development but did his best to foster it. Amte does not treat leprosy patients, tribals and other 'disabled persons' as 'objects' which are known and acted upon, but as responsible 'subjects' who know and act. He does not act upon them from outside by giving orders; he has become one with them and stimulates them from within. Only this encouragement to self - development explains how the inhabitants of Anandwan could build structures, functional and strong, without the help of architects, engineers and contractors, how they could make their fields yield more than that from the fields of their neighbours without the help of degree-holders in agriculture.

Amte's New India will do much to foster this keenness at self-development especially among the youth of the poorer and backward classes. The health of any organism depends on the vitality of each single cell. Only if all the cells of an organism are fully alive is an organism truly healthy. Amte wants his New India to be truly healthy and full of vitality. In our days it is also necessary to pay much attention to the progress of science. Amte says: "With a view to staying at one place in the era of science a man has to move with the greatest speed."

A third characteristic of the New India will be a readiness to cooperate for the common good.

Mutual cooperation for the common good is based on love, and love is the will to be one. At Anandwan no distinction is made on the ground of community, caste or creed. Hindus, Muslims, Christians, high caste and low caste, Maharashtrians, Gujaratis, Tamils and Kannadigas feel equally at home and work together in perfect harmony.

Amte himself vigorously promoted national integration through his Knit-India (Bharat Jodo) marches and through his work camps at Somnath. These camps, which comprise young people from various states, took up the Antar Bharati slogan of Sane Guruji.

The will to be one manifests itself in the readiness to cooperate for the common good. In Anandwan the profit motive is not prevalent. Workers do get an incentive pay, but most of the money earned goes to the common fund and is available for further development.

Amte's view of private property is neither that of the capitalists nor that of the communists. He says: "I believe as a society we have to evolve, through experimentation, a system which combines the principles of individual freedom and common ownership. And this is what we have tried, basically with success, in all our projects, involving leprosy patients, tribal people and the so-called 'disabled' persons."

The Fourth Characteristic of the New India: Love of Nature.

Anandwan certainly manifests a great love for nature; not only green fields are cultivated and tree planting is promoted but also the most beautiful flowers are grown there in abundance. There is even a beautiful 'monument to the unknown tree' in memory of some trees that had to be uprooted during the lay-out of the place.

But the attitude to nature is not sentimental; nature is not only admired but is also made to serve. True love of nature manifests itself in improving nature and enabling it to serve us better. Science and appropriate technology are sedulously promoted, but, at the same time, care is taken not to inflict damages on nature, especially not irreparable damage.

It is generally agreed that about one third of a country's surface should remain reserved for forests in order to preserve climatic conditions, purity of air and water supply. In India only ten per cent of the surface of the country is covered any more with primeval forests. These forests are also the natural habitat of millions of tribals. Their natural culture and their way of life are protected by the huge forests. Amte's New India will be careful to protect existing forests. Amte looks at the honey-bee as the model of what our attitude towards development should be: "Consider the honey-bee. Its treasure is nectar, obtained even from the chilli plant; it is not at the cost of the flower. In fact, its act of extracting honey contributes to the progress of the flowers. You need not learn from Khalil Gibran, Marx or Gorbachov, not even from Gandhiji. Choose instead to learn your lesson from the honey-bees as your silent partners: they will show you how to develop without destroying" (The *Illustrated Weekly of India,* Oct. 15, 1989, p. 15)

4

The Revolution Which Will Lead to a New India

When Amte was asked from where he had drawn inspiration for his work, he said: "I have, of course, been greatly influenced by the outburst of courage and awareness in the Gandhian era, and I have yearned and worked to see a resurgence in free India of a defiant and aggressive effort at self-development by the silenced majority." (*UNICEF Report,* p. 10)

What is the background to this remark?

When at the beginning of this century a number of Indian leaders had resolved to fight for India's independence, it was clear to them that they could not succeed unless they created a popular movement. If India's millions could be roused to demand independence, they were bound to succeed. They did succeed. In August 1947 India was freed from British domination. But mere political freedom was not enough. Mahatma Gandhi rightly said: "Rural swaraj will only dawn when the lowest of the low in our society will be uplifted."

To every thinking person it was obvious that a genuine inprovement in the life of the whole nation could not be achieved by government decrees and acts of parliament. A popular movement was required. The people of India would have to be roused to work for self-development with the same enthusiasm with which they fought for independence. To bring this about is what Baba Amte has yearned and worked for.

Amte believes in the potentialities inherent in the common people. He repeats over and over again: "The common man, he is the uncommon man." He admires as much the richness of heart of the common people as he despises 'the poverty of heart of the elite.'

By experience he has found that there is a divine spark in the heart of the common people, a spark that can be kindled into a mighty flame.

True revolution, therefore, has to start by rousing in the people the awareness of their capabilities. But mere awareness is not enough, people must also be given an opportunity to do something. A combination of awareness and practical work is Amte's formula for a creative revolution.

"I believe that political awareness without constructive work is impotent, and that constructive work without political awareness is equally sterile. If you must put a label to what guides my action, it would be 'creative humanism' (*UNICEF Report* p. 10).

Since the great majority of the people of India live in villages. Amte gives priority to rural development. His immediate aim is to transform the existing social organization centred on subsistence farming into a highly productive agro-industrial system. How this can be done he has shown, to some extent, in Anandwan and Somnath and he tried to spread this idea through the work-camps at Somnath to which young people from all over India are invited and he hopes to get it going through the youth villages.

Though Amte's interest is focussed primarily on rural India, what he does will be a great boon to industry as well. The increased purchasing power of the rural people will create for industry a much greater inland market.

He excludes both violent revolution and sterile criticism. He warns budding revolutionaries: "Beware, till now every revolution has devoured its children. There is a danger that tomorrow's blade of the guillotine may be smeared with your blood. Empty promises have been trampled under man's feet. A true revolution is not destructive but creative. Its face is not smeared with blood, but covered with sweat. The capitalist's dream of getting rich by exploiting the workers has lost its lustre; the blade of class-war has become blunt. All know that the workers' government had to hide its face when Solidarity gained an overwhelming victory; Mao's wrath against rural immigrants to the cities has been buried with him and his successors found a mini-skirt revolution more attractive than the Cultural Revolution. Negative slogans may appear at first more powerful, but they are short-lived, constructive movements, though they may appear weak, have a touch of lastingness."

He also rejects sterile criticism: "You cannot rouse people to awareness by placating them; tearful sighs do not create a revolution. Alms do not help to build a self-respecting community, but merely a greedy, slavish-minded herd."

The first step a creative revolution has to take is to stimulate people to work for improving their condition. Unless people's most primitive needs are satisfied they will not give you a hearing: "You cannot get a hearing from people whose stomachs are empty, nor will you find understanding in deserted homes. Stomachs must be satisfied if people are to listen to reason: there must be life in the houses for people to come to their senses."

Once the most primitive needs are satisfied, the time has come to put inspiring ideals before them: "Carry your ideals before you like banners; it is not enough to put them on pedestals. Ideals which grip the masses prove to be a mighty force. Their force is stronger than the hope of earthly gain, and they are more productive of real wealth."

Once ideals have gripped the masses, real progress is assured: "Family life will be strengthened, for homes are not made of brick and mortar, they are people united into a joint personality. Villages will be made self-supporting and will have self-rule, and this is the only way of stopping the exploitation of villages. Factories will no more be mere assemblies of living men and dead machines, but will be centres of a common effort. If seen like this the factory chimneys will not emit disgusting smoke, but the perfume of the worker's common effort.

"If revolution is creative, nationalized ownership that throttles all creative effort, will no more be the test of revolution. Participation in decision-making will stimulate workers to greater efforts and common ownership will be the aim.

"Workers and farmers will unite in a common effort and will brush aside all opposition. The war-cry will no more be with Marx and Mao: the spirit of revenge cannot build a new world. There is no substitute for Gandhi's way of rousing the impoverished masses to creative awareness" (*Karunecha Kalam,* p. 67-71).

Only a revolution which leads to a higher sense of human dignity can lead to a higher and nobler way of life. Revolutions based on hatred and violence does not really change the situation. They merely transform the people who had been exploited into a new class of exploiters but hatred and exploitation remain. Therefore, there is no substitute for Gandhi.

Rousing people to creative awareness is merely a call to people to be true to the law which is imprinted in man's heart. In the Indian tradition this law is called *sanatana dharma*. Gandhi has called it the voice of conscience, or the voice of God. It comes to the same. The traditional definition of *dharma* is: "The conscience of the virtuous who are exempted from hatred and inordinate affection" (D.F. Mulla, *Principles of Hindu Law,* p. 1).

In his book *Ujjwal Udyasathi* (For a Brighter Tomorrow) Baba Amte calls on young people to work for a New India, an India which is fully alive, and an India in which joy and contentment prevail. Amte is quite sure that from the youth of India a new and creative leadership will arise. He writes:

The new leadership in India is taking shape quietly, without any drum-beating through the newspapers. Today's newspaper loses its value tomorrow and finds its way to the waste paper basket: "These waste papers may have published the havoc played by the new generation; they may have printed about a storm blowing over the country. But remember the wheel of the windmill moves faster in a storm. Various centres, the centres of energy and strength in the life of society are gaining tremendous momentum. May be, the surging new generation of today appears to have lost its bearings, to have lost its soul. But it is absolutely certain that one day it will have its own leader and prophet. The present age is rich with new techniques, impregnated with a new constructive potential. This age will win over the destructive forces. In Japan and Germany the leadership of the new generation has rebuilt a whole nation out of ashes and sand. Perhaps we are more fortunate and have a better start than they had. I am absolutely confident that the phoenix of a new leadership is rising from the ashes of all its failures. Soon the world will witness the lightening hidden in its beak and the storm hidden in its wings" (*Ujjwal Udyasathi,* p. 50)

5

Efforts to Create a New India - 1

In the year 1964 Baba Amte developed cervical spondylosis and progressive degeneration of the spine. In 1966-67 he was confined to bed for 12 hours a day undergoing traction. In 1971 friends of Baba Amte collected money so that he could fly to London where a major operation was performed. Due to severe back pain and weakness in the lower extremities he had to observe complete bed rest in 1971-72 and had to undergo another crucial surgery in Bombay. Ever since 1964 Baba Amte is a very sick person and is constantly in pain. He cannot take a sitting posture but must either stand or lie down on a soft mattress. Normally such a state of health would spell the end of a person's public activity.

In Amte's case the many months of enforced bed rest merely provided him with the leisure required for working out detailed plans for a New India. Many illuminating ideas and insights came to his mind during these months. He said, "At first I thought my bed was a coffin, but then it became a womb." One of the children produced in this womb is the insight that the basic requirement for creating a New India is to transform the existing social organization, centred on subsistence farming, into a highly productive agro-industrial system.

In the fifties India took to planning with great enthusiasm and greater expectations. But things did not turn out as it was expected. The present development programmes, inspire of efforts to avoid it, resulted in making the rich richer and the poor poorer. An alternative programme appeared to be the need of the hour, a programme which will be a direct attack on poverty. It will not aim at giving monetary aid to the poor people but at enabling them to get out of their poverty by their own efforts. It fosters among people the growth of a creative awareness which leads to a resolute effort at self-development and at the same time shows people feasible ways of improving their condition.

Baba Amte tried to promote his idea of a New India in many different ways. He had the plan of establishing a Workers' University in order to create a highly educated generation who knows how to use their hands; he organized work camps for young people from all parts of India who would come to know new techniques and spread them. He tried to show to Adivasis the way to a productive existence. He organized a Centre of Social Action to work out the details of an alternative development. He organized the 'Bharat Jodo Abhiyan' (Knit India Marches) from Kanyakumari to Kashmir and from Assam to Gujarat in order to strengthen the sense of unity among the people of India and of late he made a heroic effort to achieve a form of development which is friendly both to nature and to people.

A Workers' University

One of the ideas conceived by Baba Amte during the long months of enforced rest was the plan of a Workers' University. It was to be a University in which students along with acquiring a degree would be trained in productive work. With their productive work students would produce enough income to make the University financially self-supporting. Not being dependent on state funds the university could develop its own programme and syllabus. The courses would include everything from science and technology to agriculture, personal hygiene and style of life. Each student would be given two acres of land to cultivate and experiment with and would be entitled to the yield of this land after paying for his board. The present universities train the mind, but the hands of the students remain incapable of doing any productive work. Farmers' sons become alienated from the village of their origin and on account of this agriculture, which is the mainstay of the Indian people, is deprived of the service of the best talents. By transforming the existing social organization, centred on subsistence farming, into a highly productive agro-industrial system, the wealth and well-being of the rural population would increase and the emigration into the cities and into the slums would cease.

With the blessing of the Planning Commission, Amte was given 2,000 acres of barren forest land at Somnath, 100 km. South of Anandwan. Amte moved into Somnath in March 1967 with Vikas, Prakash and their adopted son. Ten cured leprosy patients from Anandwan went with them. They slept in the open and began to dig a well. In April they found water. By then, however, Amte's adopted son had fallen seriously ill. He was taken to hospital at Nagpur and Sadhanatai went with him.

One day, a man from the village brought news that the boy had died. Amte set out for Nagpur immediately. The virologist who had been treating the child said he had been killed by a mysterious disease which he called simply 'the Somnath Virus'; he urged Amte to leave the area and to take the workers with him.

Back at Somnath, Amte gathered his patients together, told them what the virologist had said and added that he himself had no intention of leaving. Four or five of them, however, said bluntly, that having been cured of leprosy after so many years, they did not have the courage to face another deadly disease and walked out. When they got to the nearest village, one of the older men in the group said that they had lived through difficult and desperate times with Amte, so, why should they leave? With that they turned round, walked back to Somnath and told Amte that they were ready to live and die with him.

The following year, students from all over India came to help develop Somnath and soon twenty-five acres were under the plough. By that time, however, local opposition to the project had become intense. Why, some of the villagers demanded, had the land been given to strangers and not to their own landless labourers? The fact that nobody had been interested in the land until Amte came, was completely forgotten.

One night Amte was warned by the village policeman that a mob of about a thousand, armed with axes and stones, were setting out for Somnath with the intention of evicting him and his workers forever. He ran down through the forest to confront them before they came too near followed by some of the patients from Anandwan. As he ran, he prayed.

At one point, a narrow stream crosses the track to the village and it was there that Amte came upon the advancing mob. He shouted at them that they could cross it only over his dead body, and he sat down in their path. "Come on", he yelled, "kill me". One of his men from Anandwan, a Bihari with claw hands and ulcerous feet, bent over him protectively, like an umbrella. The policeman, who had given the alarm, urged the patients to escape while they could, but the Bihari said, "Jagdish will not run away." When he heard these words, Amte said to himself, "I am protected by the Lord in the form of this patient."

The mob wavered and one of their leaders began to harangue them, declaring that as disciples of Gandhi they believed in non-violence. When someone shouted that the police van was coming, the entire mob disappeared into the forest.

Amte had won a battle but lost a campaign. Persistent local pressure eventually forced him to hand back over 700 acres of the land which had been given to him, together with a valuable stream which would have irrigated large parts of it. It was a shattering blow, but, although he had to abandon his scheme of a workers' university, it didn't stop him and his patients from turning Somnath into a model farm. At present Somnath has about 400 inmates, most of them leprosy patients and about 1,000 out of the 1,330 acres which he was allowed to retain, are cultivated. It has become so prosperous that it can send very substantial subsidies of food and money to Anandwan.

A great difficulty was that nearly all the available water supply was lost when the 700 acres were given to the local population. Now many percolation dams have been built, which are filled with rainwater during the rainy season and their water seeps into the lower lying areas.

The profits made even now after the loss of the 700 acres show that the planned workers' university would have been economically viable.

Youth Camps

The main aim of the workers' university was to serve as an instrument to bring about a social change. It aims at transforming the existing social organization, centred on subsistence farming, into a highly productive agro-industrial system.

Though the loss of 700 acres, and with it the loss of much of the water supply, destroyed the possibility of a workers' university, Amte promoted the same plan by organizing yearly youth camps at Somnath. These camps aim at developing the personality of the participants as also at kindling the desire to work for the development of India. The thrust of Baba's speeches at these camps has been to exhort the young people to "come forward to give their 'today' for a brighter 'morrow' for the masses. He has felt that youth has a vision, vigour and a dashing spirit, but they need guidance and the joy and enthusiasm which are created by a common effort. The young people must come out of the high walls of academic life to face the realities, analyse them, to think independently and make their own decisions. The vision of a united India, as set forth by Sane Guruji, was meant to be the guiding star of this movement. In 1968, the first of these camps was started inviting youths from all over India to participate in a "production - oriented - community -action - programme."

About 1,200 young people responded to this call. They not only experienced the truth of the statement "Hands are to build, not to destroy" but also the fact of an inter-state brotherhood. They felt that the need of the hour was the knitting of hearts for a common cause, for a common purpose, to work for the upliftment of India's teeming millions.

Much of the credit for the success of this first camp goes to Dr. V.K.R.V. Rao, then Minister for Education, and Mohan Dharia who was a member of the Rajya Sabha. Both of them took active interest in Baba's ideas about the youth-work camp. Dr. Rao wrote personally to the Vice-Chancellors of all Universities to send selected teachers and students from their colleges to take part in the Somnath camp. There was an enthusiastic response from many universities which included some Agricultural Universities, the Aligarh University and the Jamia Milia Islamia of Delhi. In all 39 professors and 163 students came from 35 different Universities from all over the country.

This camp was followed by another in 1969 which involved 790 youths from Punjab, Bengal, Gujarat, Andhra Pradesh and Tamil Nadu apart from the home state Maharashtra. These camps remain an annual feature. The pattern followed in these camps is always the same.

Youths from all over India are invited to participate. In the morning they work in the fields, digging percolation dams, making bunds, clearing wasteland for cultivation, levelling agricultural land.

The day ends with discussions and group activities. Lectures by well-known speakers on topics like secularism, national integration, socialism, democracy and students' problems make these campers more aware of the malaise destroying the nation and of the need of strong-willed and dedicated workers.

Group activities involve interaction between participants in the form of songs, dances, skits, plays, poems, personal ideas and reactions. This kind of interaction brings about mutual respect and understanding and friendship and the joy of knowing people from different backgrounds and the joyful awareness of being a part of a diversely beautiful India.

Somnath has had over the years many volunteers and has brought to the fore some of the ablest youth leaders and activists. People have come to understand that the welfare state does not, and cannot, meet all human needs. That, at most, it provides us with a framework of care and protection. The rest we have to do for ourselves and for each other in the endeavour of building a New India. Working shoulder to shoulder with leprosy patients the volunteers were imbued with a greater concern for the socially disabled.

Youth Villages

In recent years campers were introduced to the idea of youth villages. Youth villages are an experiment in community living. Young people drawn from different regions and communities will live and work with the youth from the poor and underprivileged sections of the society in the neighbourhood. Such youth villages will be set up in backward areas and in poorly endowed regions inhabited by tribals or socially handicapped sections of society. On a land acquired by them they will run a farm on the scientifically most advanced methods of soil improvement, water management and rural development and by their example and non - formal education they hope to improve the life of the people in the whole region. A number of young people are preparing themselves for this work.

6

Efforts to Create a New India - 2

Hemalkasa: Lok Biradri Projects

In 1971 Amte again had trouble with his spine. Two vertebrae had to be replaced by bones taken from an animal, or, as Amte says, from an anonymous quadruped. Friends subscribed so that he could fly to London to have the operation performed there. When the London doctors learned about the work Baba Amte was doing, they performed the operation free of charge. After this very difficult operation had been performed, he had to spend two years with complete bed rest, most of the time in severe pain. This was again a time for reflection, a time in which many illuminating ideas came to him. This time also, his bed, instead of being a coffin, became a womb.

He began to reflect especially on the Madia and Gond tribes, on their living conditions. He had met them when as a young boy, on his hunting expeditions; he roamed the forest fastnesses of Central India. He was fascinated by their innocence, their cheerfulness and integrity and he was appalled by the destruction which the impact of a rapacious civilization had wrought among them. Malnutrition and diseases like rheumatism and cirrhosis of the liver were widespread. Unable yet to achieve the transition from hunting to farming they knew next to nothing and earned precious little for work done in the service of exploitative non - tribals, but they paid an artificially high price for even basic necessities like salt.

Amte conceived the magnificent idea of helping the adivasis to get integrated into modern civilization without becoming estranged from what is best in their tradition and tribal culture. He says: "My aim is to give them an education that will make them proud of their culture. These people should grow up proud of their grandfather's culture, not shunning it."

Already at Anandwan Baba had expanded his work for the leprosy afflicted to cover other categories of handicapped: the blind, the deaf, the mutes, the orthopaedically handicapped, the aged and the orphans. Now he directed his interest to the tribals, who really were his first love.

In February 1973, Baba Amte along with his son Dr. Vikas, in spite of his back ailment, scoured the area where the Adivasis lived and set up a tent at Hemalkasa 350 km. south of Nagpur. Travelling from village to village he started health work among the Madia Gonds.

The Government of Maharashtra had given to the Maharogi Seva Samiti a grant of fifty acres of land near Hemalkasa to start a centre there. Baba Amte's younger son Prakash, who had just graduated from the medical college, decided to join his father and brother. Along with 16 cured leprosy patients from Anandwan he set out for Hemalkasa and on December 24, 1974, the birthday of Sane Guruji, the Lok-Biradari-Prakalp (People's Brotherhood) was launched at Hemalkasa. It is called People's Brotherhood Project to express the intention of working not for the people but with the people by becoming one with them.

Dr. Prakash's sensitive nature responded enthusiastically to what he saw and he volunteered to take over the work. On the occasion of Baba's 60th birthday, 1974, Dr. Prakash made a declaration, as a birthday gift, that he would dedicate his life to the causes for which Baba was working. It meant giving up his work for M.S. degree, which he had just begun, and going to Hemalkasa, in the heart of the jungle, to run a small clinic for tribals.

His wife, Dr. Mandakini, a fully trained anaesthetist was a city bred girl, who had never seen a forest, but she shared her husband's adventurous, self-sacrificing spirit and responded to the situation with an amazing willingness and adaptability. Both of them determined to become one with the people in the jungle in order to help them to get integrated into the twentieth century by bringing them medical care, culture and education while preserving all that is valuable and beautiful in their original culture.

Dr. Prakash built a thatched-roof hut in a small clearing, stocked it with food and medicines and bade good-bye to the world he had known. The news that a young doctor had come who loved and cared for the people, soon spread. From far and near, on foot and by bullock carts, tribals in various stages of sickness arrived.

The situation was rather frustrating. The treatment was primitive. There was no lab of any kind, no blood, oxygen or EGG service. Electricity had not reached the region, there was no cooling device for life-saving drugs. Hemalkasa is hundred miles from Anandwan. For six months of the year it is cut off from the rest of the world by flooded rivers. No fresh vegetables are available during the rains: when the kitchen runs out of flour only rice and daal remain.

Water had to be drawn from a well, but it had a very high concentration of iron. Clothes turned orange within a week and stomachs gave trouble. Prakash became ill with an ulcer and lost 30 lbs within a few weeks. It was suggested that the project should be given up. But the Amtes are made of sterner stuff. Prakash and Mandakini stayed on.

In June 1975 his wife went to Nagpur for her first delivery. A son was born. Prakash could not be informed. There is no post or telegraph office within reach. When the flooded rivers subsided and the road became motorable, his wife and child joined him. With Dr. Mandakini at his side Prakash mustered up courage to undertake new work.

Utter poverty and ignorance are the hallmark of the tribals. Yet culturally they are sophisticated. As a craftman a tribal is superb. With a simple knife he carves the most artistic figures, and, because he is born in the arrow culture, his weapons are accurate and hard hitting.

In spite of the increasing medical work Prakash also arranged for adult literacy classes from 8 to 11 at night when the women had finished their house work and were free to attend.

Word had gone round that a boarding school for children would be started. Enthusiastic parents came with their wards and left them at the hospital. "But we are not ready to take them," Prakash's fellow workers told them. "We have not stocked food and clothing for so many." "That's your problem," argued the tribals and left. Thus, besides the school for adults, a primary school was also started.

The morning instructions follow the government syllabus. The afternoons are given to practical education in the fields. They learn to select the right kind of seed, the use of sprays, insecticides and fertilizers, vegetable culture, the various ways of watering the fields. To provide for recreation and to create a homely atmosphere there were dances, music, games, question hours and various outdoor activities.

The production of one's own food led to a more balanced diet. They also learned to calculate, demand and pay a proper price for what they sold and bought and to avoid being exploited. Better production enabled them to sell part of their produce. Better nutrition and improved hygiene resulted in fewer diseases. Thus it dawned on people that the quality of life could be improved. They began building better houses. They built a dam on the river to store water for irrigation, and a granary and finally, with the help of Swiss Aid they also built a proper hospital.

By now there are more than 250 children in the residential school. There is a well equipped hospital with 50 beds. More than 200,000 patients have been treated at Hemalkasa, many hundreds of operations have been performed. Adivasis have been trained to spread knowledge and promote progress among their own people. Eight health centres have been established which are managed by Adivasis. The people have become conscious of their rights and have learned to fight injustice and exploitation. Thus, by launching a movement with the people, for the people and by the people Dr. Prakash, Dr. Mandakini and their collaborators have brought beauty into the lives of these simple people, the beauty of health, self-respect and self-esteem.

A Threat to Tribal Life

Some 300 villages in a 100 kilometre radius have awakened to a new life. But just when a new spirit is awakening and the tribals are getting ready to adapt themselves to the world around them, their own world is threatened.

Two hydro-electric projects, the Bhopalpatnam project on the Indravati river and the Inchampalli project further down on the Godavari river threaten to submerge a large part of the land on which the Madia Gond tribals live. Baba Amte is mainly concerned with the fact that 40,000 out of the 75,000 tribals who live in that region will have to be evacuated. Some compensation is promised to them and perhaps some barren land will be allotted to them. The tribals who are so intimately connected with nature in the jungle will not be able to survive on such barren land. Baba calls this evacuation of the tribals 'cultural ethnocide'. He writes: "After my tour in the tribal belt of the Madias I feel the intensity of injustice right down to my toe-nails." Darryl D'Monte writing in *The Economist,* May 1984, p. 27, says: "It is ironical that Amte should have to face the threat of seeing the areas in which he had lived and worked being buried under tons of water to produce power for industry and to irrigate lands of rich farmers."

To avert this disaster Baba Amte, first of all, drew attention of the Prime Minister Indira Gandhi to the situation. On 12th July, 1983, he wrote the following letter:

Dear Smt. Indiraji,

This concerns a matter that has been disturbing me deeply for some time. I did not think it proper to mention it during your visit to Anandwan last year. And I could not write earlier as I was away the last three months in a Bombay hospital.

I now write to seek your intervention in the government move to construct the Inchampalli hydel project on the Godavari and the Bhopalpatnam hydel project on the Indravati. I do so knowing how sensitive you are, personally and as Prime Minister, to questions relating to forest wealth and tribal life and culture.

Very briefly the facts are as follows:

Between the two projects some 2, 00,000 acres of land will be submerged - nearly half of it prime forest, dense, mixed and deciduous. As you know, the country today has much less than the desirable third of the land under forest cover and even this reduced proportion is dwindling in the name of development. I would suggest that we have to generate electricity without seriously encroaching on our forests. I believe this would be possible. For example the coal deposits in the Pranhita valley could be tapped for thermal power.

Likewise, it might not be necessary to incur the multiple costs and risks in building more dams of a gigantic size. A series of smaller dams could, I submit, adequately meet the water and energy needs of the people, including electricity for industry, without degrading the environment. My discussions with government technocrats familiar with this region strengthen this view.

Once costs and benefits are fully reckoned, it should be possible to see the economic and ecological implications of a project as part of a composite picture. The present and future costs of destroying cultivable land and forests (neither of which can be recreated) are evidently more than the benefits of the expected electricity and water (for which alternative means could be found).

There is another more poignant aspect to the proposed Inchampalli and Bhopalpatnam projects. The forests they will submerge are the homeland of the Madia Gond tribal people.

At least 40,000 tribal persons will be uprooted, along with the loss of millions of trees. Of course, it is intended to transplant these people elsewhere with the help of some monetary compensation. But nothing can compensate the wrench they would suffer in leaving their traditional cultural environment for an alien Marathi speaking setting. Today, the Madia Gond tribals maintain their struggle for survival only because of the life support system that the forests provide. There is also a value system that sustains tribal life which is rooted in the struggle and sharing honour and honesty. It is nature that nurtures these values. To remove the tribal people from their natural habitat would be cultural 'ethnocide' apart from adding to their adversity. I need hardly mention the many endangered species of rare and precious animals.

I would earnestly request you to intercede on behalf of Man and Nature, and reaffirm the national policy of protecting forest wealth and tribal culture. Such a policy is, I am sure, the best guarantee against present problems and future shocks.

Specifically I would like to seek.

(a) An interim stoppage of work on the ground in pursuit of the two projects by Central or any of the three state governments: Maharashtra, Andhra and Madhya Pradesh.

(b) A statement of national policy clarifying priorities in human, social and ecological terms in the context of economic development.

(c) An investigation into alternative means and methods of supplying water and energy for the region.

I would be thankful to hear from you soon. With my esteem and personal regards,

Yours truly,
(Baba Amte)

Here is the cryptic reply he received from the Prime Minister:

New Delhi,
August 30, 1983

Dear Shri Amte,

I have received your letter of July 12, 1983 regarding the Inchampalli and Bhopalpatnam projects. My own views are well known. But it is a very difficult battle. We shall pursue this matter. I am asking the Planning Commission to look very carefully into the aspects you have mentioned.

Yours sincerely,
Indira Gandhi

Baba Amte wrote to Indira Gandhi again on June 24, 1984 and to Rajiv Gandhi in the following year, September 20, 1985 and received the same polite and non-committal replies.

Besides informing the Government, Amte began to organize opposition among the tribals themselves. On April 9, 1984 thousands of tribals made a morcha presenting a memorandum to the collector to be forwarded to Mrs. Gandhi urging her to call off the project. Sundarlal Bahuguna, of Chipko Andolan, who took part in the morcha said he had never seen such a huge crowd of tribals assembled to express their opinion.

In an interview with Pritish Nandy of the *Illustrated Weekly of India,* May 20, 1984, Baba Amte declared : "Our problem is actually quite simple : We cannot allow the tribals to be culturally uprooted, to be exploited in the name of progress and that is why they will build these dams over my dead body. Not just me, the tribals will resist this. They will form human chains. Women and children will cling to the trees. Let's see, how ruthless the State can be."

Baba Amte and his co-workers made careful studies showing up glaring miscalculations in the cost-profit ratio on which the projects are based. For instance they point out that the project planners take into account only the value of the standing timber in an area that is to be submerged and not the recurring annual yield which can be enhanced by proper management. For instance: according to Col. Verma of AFPRO (Action for Food Production) the loss of 40,000 hectares of forest will total over 2,500 crores as against an absurdly low figure of 9 crores as estimated by the Maharashtra Forest Department which values it at Rs 2,000 per hectare.

What Baba Amte is really fighting for is the future of India, the future of the people of India: Should we aim at the welfare of the people as a whole with special regard to the weak and underprivileged, or shall we allow a development to continue by which the rich become richer and the poor become poorer. Should development aim at satisfying the greed of a powerful clique or the needs of the common people.

Because of opposition to the dam and on account of financial difficulties work on the two dams has been suspended and a final decision has been postponed to the Seventh Five Year Plan.

New Knit India March (Bharat Jodo Abhiyan)

Baba Amte was much disturbed by observing the disrupting forces in the form of regionalism, communalism, casteism that have been thriving in India since independence. Turbulent happenings in the country during the late seventies and early eighties have made every thinking person in India restless. Finally the November riots in Delhi and North India and the ugly incidents throughout the country would not allow him to sit quiet. He felt conflicts had reached a point of explosion and in any other country such a state of affairs would have led to an armed revolt. He saw the country in agonizing pain; blood was oozing from its wounds in the Punjab, in Assam, Gujarat and elsewhere.

To remain an idle spectator in such a situation was against his conscience. Baba is deeply convinced of the truth of Burke's famous statement: "For evil to triumph, it is only necessary for the good men to do nothing." But what could he do?

The youth camps at Somnath had brought young people together from all parts of India. The idea of 'Knit India', the idea of promoting unity in India had been born there. Amte has great confidence in young people. He feels that among the youth of India a new leadership is quietly taking shape. Thus the idea of Bharat Jodo Abhiyan began to take shape. The young people he had come to know at Somnath could form the nucleus of a group that would march from Kanyakumari to the Himalayas, from Assam to Gujarat, promoting the desire for oneness, promoting the awareness of belonging together among the people of various states and communities.

Would it be worthwhile? Would they achieve something by this mighty effort? When Mahatma Gandhi undertook the salt march the little salt he picked up at Dandi did not immediately establish the independence of India, but it did start a movement which led to India's independence. "Whatever be the outcome", Amte said, "I am out to do my bit to cure the malady."

Preparation for the March

This long march by cycle needed meticulous planning and organization. The plans were chalked out in the annual Youth Camp at Somnath in May 1985. Steps were taken to register the Bharat Jodo Abhiyan Samiti. Enthusiastic calls, inquiries and applications started pouring in, which were sorted out and participants chosen.

The criteria for selection were simple and unbiased. The participants were to be in the age group of 21-35 and be able to travel on a two-wheeler (cycle or moped) over long distances.

Those with the ability to stage street plays, to lead group songs etc. were to be preferred. Participants were expected to lead a disciplined community life during the march. The organizers had expected to get three to four participants from each state. The group that was actually formed had a preponderance of youths from southern and western India and only a sprinkling from the north and north-eastern regions.

The march itself had to be carefully prepared. Local committees all along the way had to arrange for food and shelter for the participants' short stay and organize public meetings. Permission had to be obtained from the various states for interstate movement of vehicles participating in the march. Money required for food and shelter was collected by the local committees through the sale of Jodo Badges, stickers, diaries, T-shirts, posters and banners.

The March Itself

The march started at Kanyakumari on 24th December 1985, the birth anniversary of Sane Guruji and ended in Jammu on 9th April 1986 the day on which 44 years ago Mahatma Gandhi had issued his 'Quit India' call to the British. They actually travelled 5,250 km (instead of the planned 5042 km) in 107 days (95 cycling days, 12 rest days). The average distance covered per day was 53 km. There were in all 110 participants including 16 girls. Many students, NSS volunteers and other joined them. Some accompanied them up to the boundary of their state, some for shorter distances.

In many places they received an enthusiastic reception. Baba Amte addressed the people and implored them to work for the unity and integrity of India and for the preservation of their surroundings. He exhorted them especially to plant trees. Everywhere he told them: "Raise your hands for construction, not to beg or destroy. Raise your hands in unity so that there will be forest of hand to build a New India." The most enthusiastic response Baba got in Maharashtra, in tribal areas, and by the Sikh community especially in places like Indore which had witnessed some of the worst killings during the 1984 riots. As the marchers turned towards the North the mood changed.

The euphoria and expectancy evaporated as they faced hard facts about Indian life, when they saw the poverty, misery and injustice which the poor people had to endure, when they began to sense the fear and anguish in the minds of the people living closer to Punjab, the wrath, pain and suffering of the affected Punjabis and a lot more.

Amte insisted throughout: "Bharat Jodo is not an end in itself. It is only a starting point." Indeed it was meant to rekindle something of the patriotic fervour which had gripped the masses during the Independence struggle. One plan fully matured during the march, the idea of Youth villages. Participants in the march were the first to volunteer to be trained at Somnath for carrying out this plan.

The second Knit India march from Itanagar in Assam to Okha in Gujarat started in November 1988 and ended in April 1989. Everywhere Amte took keen interest in the condition of the people. Giving his impression of the North East he states:

"I think our march is particularly relevant for the North-East and we have also learned much during our march. I sense a change in the mood of the tribal people here. Some of them might once have engaged in secessionist activities, but I am convinced that phase is over. They want to remain a part of India. During my march, at times, I have felt whether I am really in India, a democratic country, or in a country under military rule... I have also been struck by the fact that there has been very little development, though much money is being spent. And what little development has taken place, its benefits have not percolated to the poor at the bottom. For instance, till now I have seen only one biogas plant on my travels. Even the Christian missionaries have concentrated their efforts almost exclusively on education. Well, perhaps also health care. But no other development work has been done even by them. For instance, little has been done to wean the tribal people away from the destructive practice of slash and burn cultivation. If the practice continues before long we may have a "Great Himalayan Desert" in the region" (*Frontline,* December 10- 23, 1988).

The final experience of the participants in the two marches: "We who were strangers to each other three months ago, can become friends in spite of our differences; is it impossible for love and friendship to prevail amongst our countrymen who have lived and shared India's past and present?" To create the desire for such friendship and to prove that such friendship is possible, was the main purpose of these marches.

Peace Missions to the Punjab

The steadily deteriorating situation in the Punjab distressed Baba Amte very much. During his 'Knit-India' March he had come to know the agony, fear and anxiety which gripped both Hindus and Sikhs. He wanted to be with them in these dark days. Six times he went to the Punjab and talked to both Sikhs and Hindus. He knew that he was on the hit list of the extremists, but he travelled through the most affected areas and refused police protection. When reporters asked him "What brought you back to the Punjab?" he replied, "The love and affection of the people. I want the sufferings of the Punjabis to end as fast as possible." When asked what he suggested for bringing peace to the state, he said "What is needed is the healing touch and this is what government has to do." To the question: in what way the healing touch could be provided, he replied: "During the past four weeks I have met lakhs of people in different districts of the Punjab... The conclusions I have come to after my deliberations: the government must release the innocent among the Jodhpur detenus. It should hasten the proceedings against those involved in the Delhi riots and compensation must be given to the victims of all types of violence in and outside the Punjab. A popular government could also be restored to the State." (*Hindustan Times,* Sept. 26, 87).

7

Narmada Bachao

Wherever there is a group of people afflicted by severe suffering or threatened by extinction Baba Amte feels irresistibly drawn towards them. Towards the end of his life Baba Amte's attention was drawn to the fate of 30,000 Adivasis who were to be deprived of their home, who were to be driven from the land which they had cultivated for centuries.

How Baba Amte's Attention was drawn to the Narmada Valley Project

During his struggle to save the Madia Gonds from being driven out of their forests by the Inchampalli and Bhopalpatnam projects Amte had become aware of the problems involved in India's development policy and his attention was drawn to the Narmada vally project, a gigantic project involving an expense of more than 11,000 crores of rupees by which 44,363 hectares of fertile land and 40,332 hectares of India's best natural forest will be submerged and nearly 3,00,000 people will be ousted from their villages, most of them tribals.

Along with several hundred important environment activists Baba Amte began to study the implications of this project. The more they studied it the clearer it was seen that the Narmada valley project is an outstanding example of the form of development, which, acting on the profit motive, destroys nature and endangers the future of the human race.

In order to arouse a nation-wide awareness of the implications of the Narmada valley project, Baba Amte arranged a meeting of prominent environment activists at Anandwan in the first week of July 1987. Another meeting to discuss ways and means of opposing the destruction of India's natural wealth was held at Hemalkasa in May 1988. It was realized that such local meetings could do little to rouse a nation-wide awareness of the danger threatening India by gigantic dams. A big meeting would have to be organized which would give a signal to the nation and to the world. Thus the idea originated of organizing a meeting at Harsud, a town in the Narmada valley, which will be submerged by the Sardar Sarovar Project. The final decision to go ahead with organizing the Harsud Rally was taken in Itarasi at a meeting held on August 10 and 11, 1989 in which 60 organizations from all over India participated. After the second 'Knit-India Yatra' which had ended in April 1989, Baba Amte had returned to Anandwan very weak, with severe anaemia and heart problems. On September 19 he slipped and fell down fracturing his left hand which had to be put into plaster. In spite of all these health problems and against medical advice Baba Amte travelled to Harsud to address the rally on September 28, 1989.

The Impact of the Harsud Rally

The Harsud Rally brought together the organizational skill of the Green Network matching them with the enthusiasm of the tribals and peasants from far and near who protested against being displaced. Also a number of international environment networks pledged their support. A green front had miraculously emerged for the first time in the nation's history.

The Harsud Rally and its message were not only prominently reported in the Indian press, radio and television, but also the international media participated in full strength. Harsud got three minutes time in the BBC news report, Time and The National Geographic Magazine were there to make sure that Harsud would become known as the common man's protest against the destruction of nature.

At the end of the rally Baba Amte administered the Harsud pledge to the assembled people, the pledge to halt destructive dams by using non-violent means. Shabana Azmi, the famous actress and champion of the cause of slum dwellers, pointed out that uprooting people from their cultural surroundings merely means increasing the population of the slums. Baba Amte said: "Mohandas Karamchand Gandhi wrote: 'The Indian village, like a woman, carries the future of the nation in its womb.' Yet our government is preparing to wipe 500 Indian villages from the face of the earth. No one is allowed to arrange for the funeral of the future."

On September 28, 1989 the nation's planners, the World Bank and industrial interests found themselves facing the prospect of encountering new waves of opposition to their plans.

Attempts at achieving a Dialogue with Government

In the opening pages of his booklet *Cry, the Beloved Narmada* Baba Amte writes:

A national obligation compels me to speak to the people of India. In September last year (1988) over 300 citizens, comprising many of the most distinguished Indians of this era, submitted to the Prime Minister a memorandum on the Narmada Valley Project. The memorandum outlines a carefully documented case for undertaking a thorough reappraisal of the Narmada Valley Project (NVP). In my forwarding letter to the Prime Minister I wrote: "This is an expression of a truly collective national will by a large number of people and organizations... They are the voice of the nation. I would urge you to pay the most careful heed to the questions they have raised, the suggestions they have offered."

"When I look back at the last nine months, however, I can feel only deep pain and disappointment at the manner in which the Government has responded. Far from taking the lead in promoting an open and well-informed debate on the issue, the Government has taken every conceivable step to crush the very possibility of a meaningful dialogue. Its spokesmen have carried on a massive campaign of disinformation and misrepresentation regarding the essential facts of the project as well as the motivation and standpoint of those raising questions about it."

Immediately after the memorandum was submitted, a virtual tirade was launched against the signatories...

"What is worse, the Government clamped the official Secrets Act of 1923 upon the Sardar Sarovar Project (SSP).

"On October 18, 1988 twelve villages at the dam site, which were to be submerged by it, inhabited by thousands, were declared "prohibited places" under the Act.

"As wave after wave of popular protest followed at the dam site, the Official Secrets Act was invoked to arrest, harass and abuse the activists. Particularly worthy of mention is the totally non-violent demonstration of February 22, 1989, in which nearly 10,000 people from the submergence areas of Madhya Pradesh, Maharashtra and Gujarat marched to the dam site. Completely unprepared for and unnerved by this massive show of people's power the police resorted to brutal methods and even man - handled female activists, including their tireless leader Medha Patkar. These actions must be seen in the context of the reported readiness of the Chief Minister of Gujarat to bring out troops if necessary to crush the rising crescendo of protests against the dam." (*Cry, the Beloved Narmada* pp. 1-2)

When the National Front Government came into power Baba Amte tried once more to open a dialogue with Government by writing a letter to Prime Minister V.P. Singh, a letter which was signed by many prominent persons. In this letter he wrote:

Dear Shri. V.P. Singh,

The assumption of office by the National Front Government under your leadership has rekindled a sense of hope in the minds of millions of people in India. Personally you are seen as an embodiment of genuine commitment in the fight against *dhanatantra* and *bhrashtachar* which have become the very hallmarks of our body politic. You have pledged to make the voice of your government the voice of the millions of Indian homes that are without the light of hope. You have promised us an open government which does not flinch at the critical glance of the people. The National Front is seen as being committed to a development strategy based on the cardinal principles of decentralization of power and self-reliance...

We write to you today on an issue of the greatest national significance which goes to the heart of each of the major concerns to which you have pledged your government.

Then he explains the need for a review of the NVP and ends thus his letter saying:

Dear Prime Minister, the government that preceded yours completely failed to keep its commitment towards furthering a process of dialogue. We have greater expectation from you. You must break this icy silence and go to the people. We appeal to you to come forth and take the initiative to immediately open talks with the Narmada Bachao Andolan, which has become the embodiment of the struggle of the people of the Narmada valley. Looking forward to an urgent effective response from you,

Yours sincerely,
Baba Amte

Yet no effective response came. Baba Amte therefore felt obliged to address the people of India and to inform them of what was at stake in the NVP. He did this in a number of ways:

In July 1989 he published his booklet *Cry, the Beloved Narmada*. March 1990 he published a booklet entitled *The Case against the Narmada Project and Alternative Perspectives.*

In April 1990 he wrote a number of articles in the *Economic and Political Weekly* on the Narmada Project: 'The case against and alternative perspectives' *(Economic and Political Weekly,* Vol 25, n.16, April 21, 1990).

The main arguments which Baba Amte brings against the NVP are the following:

The claims on which the project is based are a blatant lie:

The Sardar Sarovar Project (SSP) has been hailed as the lifeline of Gujarat, as the permanent solution of the water problem of Saurashtra and Kutch, as the panacea for all of Gujarat's drought-prone and arid areas. Yet a careful examination of data supplied by government shows that of the 69 talukas of Saurashtra as many as 56, i.e. 81 per cent, will not get any water from the SSP; in Kutch 5 out of the 9 talukas will not get any water.

According to official estimates there are 43 drought-prone and 8 arid talukas in Gujarat. Out of these 51 talukas, as many as 30 will not get a drop of water from the SSP. Only 17 out of the 51 drought-prone or arid talukas of Gujarat will get significant amounts of water from the project.

Baba Amte adds that about half of the water supplied by the SSP goes to the districts of Ahmedabad, Baruch, Vadodara, Kheda, where an overwhelming proportion of Gujarat's water resources are already concentrated. Suren Chowksi, president of the Central Gujarat Chamber of Commerce is reported as having stated: "The prosperity of Gujarat depends on the Sardar Sarovar Project. We need electricity for the sugar mills and the new industries." In these words the main purpose of the SSP appears to be adequately stated. Half of the water supplied by the SSP goes to industrialist and r-ich farmers whilst most of the people living in drought-prone or arid talukas get no water.

The Unbearable Financial Burden for Gujarat

The official estimate of the total financial cost of the SSP is Rs. 11.154 crores (at 1987-88 prices). Gujarat has to raise 900 crores a year. The budgetary deficit of the State of Gujarat has been rising steadily and is expected to reach a record of Rs. 600 crores this year (1990). What hope can Gujarat have to allocate 900 crores each year for the SSP?

The excessive preoccupation with this one project will lead to the neglect of other vital concerns and will render it impossible to finance irrigation projects for the drought-prone areas which do not get a drop of water from the SSP.

Submergence of agricultural land and forests

According to official statistics 1, 30,482 hectares of land will be submerged by the project, of which 55,681 ha are mostly prime-quality agricultural land and 56,060 ha are forest land, some of the best rain-forest land still left in India.

According to the Department of Environment and Forests the environmental cost of the loss of forests due to the NVP would be Rs. 39,113 crores. Baba Amte notes: "So terrified are the project authorities of the devastating implications of these estimates that we have been denied all access to the relevant data and calculations and all discussions on this issue have been firmly suppressed by the government."

Large Scale Cultural Ethnocide

Baba Amte notes: "Finally and above all, I oppose this project for the large scale ethnocide: Three lakhs of people living in the submergence zone will be rendered homeless by this project."

Already more than 50,000 living in the place where the foundations of the SSP dam were dug have been expelled with nowhere to go. The people of the Narmada Valley with their long experience of talks with officials spread over many years at every level have come to the conclusion that a just resettlement is impossible, whatever be the claims, promises and paper policies of the government.

Meanwhile, the endlessly prolonged atmosphere of uncertainty has brought all developmental activity in these areas to a standstill, with the spectre of submergence looming large on the horizon.

An Alternative Approach

An alternative plan should start with a development plan for the people of the Narmada Valley instead of destroying the living conditions of its people and it should aim at improving all the drought-prone regions of Gujarat. Canal-irrigation, at its best, can reach only 40 per cent of the cultivable ground.

An intense promotion of watershed projects, dry-farming and smaller dams is the way of improving the whole of the agricultural ground.

The Jayant Patel Independent Review Group appointed by the Centre – and prevented from even visiting Gujarat – has received more than 10 proposals of alternative plans from such sources as two former chief irrigation engineers of Madhya Pradesh. One plan worked out by Mr. Suhas Paranjape, an engineer and social worker, reduces submergence by 70 per cent, the number of affected villages by 80 to 90 per cent and increases the water supply to Kutch five-fold. Details of this plan were published in the *Times of India* on August 11, 1994.

Baba Amte leaves Anandwan for Narmada

Since it became evident that the Government of Gujarat with all its power opposed a review of the NVP, the fate of the nearly 300,000 tribals living in the valley appeared to be inevitable: they would lose the land they had cultivated for many generations and would be driven away from their homes.

Wherever there is a group of people afflicted by severe suffering Baba Amte feels irresistibly drawn towards them. When the sight of a dying leprosy patient lying naked in the rain revealed to him the fate of many thousand leprosy patients he decided to become one with them and to devote his life to their uplift. Now when he had come to know the fate of the tribals living in the forests in the Narmada valley he felt an increasing urge to become one with them and to share their fate.

The work which he had started among the leprosy patients could go on without him. His son Dr. Vikas and his wife Dr. Bharati not only carried on the work most efficiently but had even introduced a number of significant improvements.

He, therefore, decided to leave Anandwan and to settle down among the tribals of the Narmada valley. He also realised that his stay in the Narmada Valley would be the strongest possible appeal to government and development agencies like the World Bank to reconsider their development policies: to give up a policy that leads to the destruction of nature and people and to aim at the sufficiency of all before working for the superfluity of some.

Amte always points to the honeybee as the model of what our attitude towards development should be: "Consider the honeybee. Its treasure is nectar obtained even from the chilli plant, yet not at the cost of the flower... Learn your lesson from the honeybees, they will show you how to develop without destroying."

When Amte was considering whether he should decide to live with leprosy patients Sadhanatai encouraged him saying: "You must follow the dictate of your conscience, I shall find my happiness in following you." Now again she said, "I shall find my happiness in following you," and she decided to accompany him to the Narmada and, if the hour came, to die with him.

Baba said: "Now when the sun of my life is about to set, I have set out to catch the rising sun of environmental awareness in this country. My presence at the Narmada river will be enough. The sound of my silence will be enough to help people to hear the cry of the Narmada.

"The moment has come for me to leave Anandwan, the place where I made my beginning into the world of joy, the place that symbolizes the very meaning of my existence. I am leaving to live along the Narmada... to attain a peace that all mankind desires. The struggle for a New India is taking place in the Narmada valley. Today the Narmada valley has become the arena for a new imagination and creativity, for a society in which there must be sufficiency for all before there is superfluity for some.

"Let me call upon each of you to become part of this glorious vision... Narmada will linger on the lips of the nation as a symbol of all struggles against social injustice."

Baba Amte and Sadhanatai settled down at Kasarvad, Khargaon District in Madhya Pradesh, in a little house built for him by the Adivasis. His daily schedule was: getting up at 5.30, going for a walk with Tai, visiting villages, lunch, taking rest and watching the Narmada flow past, discussing the dam with journalists, industrialists, T.V. reporters, speaking to farmers and politicians, garnering support for the movement and writing to various journals, and, he adds, "Doing a little bit of exercise for my back." Asked what he did most evenings he replied: "Watch the last rays of the sun kiss the Narmada giving it an orange glow, read a little and retire."

An Attempt to Force Amte to Leave the Place

Soon after Baba Amte had settled down, the authorities installed loudspeakers at the temporary police post quite close to Amte's place and played film-songs day and night at top volume. Omprakash Raval, a social worker and staunch supporter of Baba filed a writ petition at the Indore High Court against the State Government, the Khargaon District Collector and Superintendent of Police under I.P.C. 225, stating that the loudspeakers were installed to unnecessarily harass and disturb the peace of mind of Baba Amte. Justice R.K. Varma and Justice S.D. Shah of Madhya Pradesh High Court ordered the Dt. Collector, Khargaon, to personally make inquiries and inform the High Court within a week's time. Having received information that the loudspeakers had been installed without any reason in close vicinity of Baba Amte's hut and prevented Baba Amte from getting any sleep for days together and that this had a bad effect on his health, the Bench ordered the Collector to remove the loudspeakers without delay.

The Templeton Award

A number of things happened after Baba Amte settled at the Narmada which increased 'the sound of his silence' and helped people to hear the 'cry of the Narmada'. The most important of these events, was the conferring of the Templeton Award. At the very time Baba Amte had decided to settle at the Narmada he was informed that he and the Australian C.L. Birch were named for the Templeton Award. The Templeton Award was established in 1972 by financier John Templeton for 'Progress in Religion'. Templeton kept the amount of the Templeton Award higher than the Nobel Prizes in the belief that religion was more important. The value of the Templeton Award was US$ 6, 84,000. In his reply to the Templeton Trust Baba Amte wrote that it was an honour for him to have been chosen for this award; however he regretted that he was not able to travel to London to receive the award on account of his commitment to the people of the Narmada valley. "I cannot bear," he wrote, "to be away till a new hope dawns for the people of the Narmada valley." He would send his son Dr. Vikas Amte, who was now the Director of Anandwan, to attend the presentation ceremony at Buckingham Palace on May 8. He also added that this award was a tribute to the spirit of the people who worked with him. The news that Baba Amte had been given the Templeton Award reached people in all countries and continents and people everywhere began enquiring about the cause that prevented him from leaving the people of the Narmada valley even for a short time.

The 'Right Livelihood Award'

Another event which increased Baba Amte's 'sound of silence' and focused the attention of environmentalists the world over on the problems involved in the Narmada Project, was the conferment of 'The Right Livelihood Award' 1991, on Baba Amte and Medha Patkar.

The 'Right Livelihood Award,' established by the Swedish-German writer Jakob von Uexkull, carries prize money of 17,000 US dollars and is considered a Nobel equivalent in ecology and protection of nature.

Count Arthur Tarnowski, London had made a determined effort to see that the Nobel Peace Prize, 1991 was awarded to Baba Amte. To achieve his purpose he had made Amte's work and the purpose of his settling down at the Narmada known to all politically and culturally influential people in Europe and the USA. He did not succeed in this, but as a result of his efforts the Right Livelihood Prize, which is also called the Alternative Nobel Prize was awarded to Baba Amte and Medha Patkar. Medha Patkar is a social activist who together with Baba Amte fights for the protection of the Adivasis whose existence is threatened by the Narmada Project. The bestowing of this Prize on Baba Amte and Medha Patkar made the controversy about the Narmada Project known worldwide.

The Long March, December 25, 1990 till January 4, 1991

On December 25, 1990 about 5,000 tribals gathered at Badvani in the Western part of Madhya Pradesh to march 250 km to the Sardar Sarovar dam to move the Gujarat Government to review the whole project. This march was organized as a last resort after the breakdown of talks between Baba Amte and the Gujarat Development Minister Babubhai Patel.

The Gujarat Government tried to persuade the Madhya Pradesh Government to arrest the marchers, but J.S. Mathur, Collector of Shalna District in Madhya Pradesh, said he would not allow police action on the marchers within the state.

The next plan of the Gujarat Government was to collect about 50,000 pro-dam agitators to confront the anti-dam marchers at the Gujarat-Madhya Pradesh border so that it would appear that it was not the government but the people of Gujarat that opposed the anti-dam agitation.

The Gujarat Government also posted nearly 2,000 policemen and women at Ferkua the border village to guard the border. Though the government made every effort to gather many thousands of pro-dam agitators, brought them there by buses, supplied them with ample food and kept a medical officer there looking after their needs, not many pro-dam agitators could be persuaded to remain in Ferkuva. It was the cold season and to be exposed in the open to a morning temperature of 3°C was too much for people without a real motivation. The anti-dam agitators knew what they were fighting for and were ready to endure any hardship.

The anti-dam marchers and the police faced one another for several days. The police were reluctant to take action because of the presence of many people from the electronic and print media.

When finally on January 4 the marchers tried to break through the police cordon the police cracked down on Baba and his followers and arrested 125 of them. The marchers strictly stuck to non-violence, having their hands tied behind their backs, in spite of the rough and inhuman treatment inflicted on them. Baba himself physically broke down under this rough treatment, and fell unconscious. He suffered a heart attack. He was refused medical treatment as he insisted on being arrested before being taken to a hospital.

On being informed about the situation Dr. Vikas Amte and his brother Dr. Prakash rushed to Ferkuva and Dr. Prakash took Baba to a hospital at Indore where he had to undergo an operation and a pace-maker was inserted. Baba Amte returned the Padmashri and Padma Vibhusan Awards to the President of India in protest against the inhuman treatment.

The Statesman in its editorial of January 8, 1991 reports:

"Baba Amte's illness and the rough treatment reportedly meted out to him on the Gujarat-Madhya Pradesh border, further highlights the dangerous confrontation that seems to be building up over the Sardar Sarovar dam. The earlier police crackdown at Ferkuva, which made a mockery of Mr. Chimanbai Patel's carefully worked out policy of engineering a showdown between those for and against the Narmada project was one more proof of the unreliability of the State machinery when it comes to organizing or counter-organizing an agitation. Even the fire-and-brimstone political campaign that Mr. Patel launched with the entire Gujarat language press behind it has not helped to raise more than a handful of people to challenge the 5000 strong anti-dam agitators. The Gujarat Government can in no way justify its decision to seal the border with thousands of armed policemen to prevent unarmed agitators from marching through the State with hands tied in a symbolic gesture of non-violence."

A Healing Mission to Riot - Torn Mumbai

Baba Amte told a friend:

"My first pacemaker was not co-operating with me so I had to have it removed and another implanted. When I returned from the hospital in Indore to the banks of Narmada, some foreign visitors who were camping there switched on the BBC news. We heard that the first dome of the Babri Masjid had been pulled down, then the second, then the third. I began to worry where we were heading as a nation. That night I was convulsed with worrisome thoughts. I had quietly watched as chaos broke out and no political party or person was in a position to bring back harmony.

"My blood pressure began rising steadily, the doctors were helpless as their medication showed no success. At this juncture it was my wife who correctly diagnosed my ailment and said: 'Baba is very restless because he has Ayodhya BP.' Since there was no medicine for this BP I decided to rush into the arena and not to watch passively from the banks of the Narmada."

When leaving for Mumbai he issued an appeal to the Nation which was printed in many papers:

"I am setting out on what God may deem the last and most important pilgrimage of my life, a journey into the hearts and minds of the people of India. The blinding haze of dust raised by the demolition of a mosque in Ayodhya forces me to break my self- imposed exile on the banks of the Narmada. Today at the age of 79 I pray to God that my disobedient, broken body obeys the compelling dictates of my conscience.

"My opposition to the construction of large destructive dams on the Narmada will remain to my last breath. But today I must set out to dam the enormous river of tears that the devastation in and after Ayodhya has unleashed.

"All that we cherished and lived by, the unassailable spirit of oneness that invigorated us, that carried this great nation through the sternest of challenges has been delivered a deathblow. It is as if the soul of the nation had died. This spirit has to be rebuilt, renewed, and revived.

"Today I want to ask you: Is it right for us to make the weak and innocent die for what we consider to be the mistakes of history? An enormous challenge beckons all those who take pride in the glorious tradition of India's civilization; let us come together to remove every trace of hatred from the hearts of our people. Let us say a firm and unyielding 'NO' to those who try to divide us in the name of religion. Let us resolve never to be part of this cycle of retribution and revenge.

"Let us build at the disputed site in Ayodhya, neither, mandir nor masjid, but a true temple of love, our own gift to the orphaned in this mad violence, a place where they could receive tender care and wholesome upbringing. Let Ayodhya become a symbol of human brotherhood and unity, of tolerance and love, of the oneness of the spirit which is the true essence of all religion...."

When Baba accompanied by Sadhanatai, reached Bombay he was aghast to see the carnage and the intense communal hatred. He writes: "The night the fire broke out in Behrampada, I rushed there and was personally witness to the people laying themselves in the path of the fire-engine obstructing it from reaching the spot.

"I wanted to settle down in the riot affected area for a few days to infuse new confidence in those refugees who are returning home. Instead of giving in to the people who say that Muslims should be moved to Muslim majority areas and Hindus should be settled in Hindu dominated areas, people should be encouraged to return to their original neighbourhood. Dividing the two communities will only deepen the chasm.

"I wanted to go and stay with my wife at the Behrampada slum merely to convince people and the citizens of nearby Kherwadi, that the place was quite safe. I wanted to set an example in Bombay by staying in the most disturbed area before going back to the Narmada, and thus to go on a creative adventure for bringing mutual love, trust and affection.

"I was touched seeing the way the people of Dharavi went about bringing back their neighbours who had fled one morning to refugee camps because they were victims of fundamentalist forces. They did so without rushing to government for help or seeking the help of social workers... They brought back all 29 families though curfew was still in force in their area. The immense, intense love for their neighbours which I witnessed there I have never seen anywhere in India.

"My mission to Bombay is not for a week or two. It is a mission to get the silent majority to listen to the promptings of their conscience. I am worried about the silent majority of this country. It is this majority that is my hope, my only hope. I went to them, talked to them and said that if they remain silent now they are in danger of becoming a silenced majority with fascism making a bold thrust."

(*The Sunday Observer*, People, February 21 - February 27 1993)

On leaving Bombay Baba Amte issued the following appeal to the people of India:

"As I leave Bombay to return to my old struggle on the banks of the Narmada I reach out and touch the silent majority through these lines once more.

"The silent majority, who looked with dismay and anguish at the violence unleashed and were terrified by the deep divisions caused among people, are the source of my inspiration, courage and joy, for it is they who will ultimately decide the course of history and the healing process.

"I, therefore, reach out and am among them in brotherhood and sisterhood and in struggle, and urge them to relentlessly combat, without compromise of conscience, the forces of division and hatred; to resist the evil forces of communalism, whether Hindu or Muslim, in the offices, on the streets, in the courts, in the schools and factories and, most important, at home.

"To tear apart the fabric of lies of the rabid communalists who use history to mislead and culture to deceive. Be wary of those who use religion – the universal language of peace to wage war.

"Particularly, protect the women and children who have been the victims of the 'ethnic cleansing' that has taken place.

"To the youth of India: Work among the people. They will test you before they trust you, therefore work selflessly and relentlessly striving to rebuild this great cosmopolitan city, but also to be a beacon for the rest of the country to know that India can be great without weapons and war, if its people are happy and at peace with themselves. And to my brothers in the police force, many of whom have gone astray – you foremost have the power to protect lives. May God give you strength never again to waver from the path of duty."

Baba Amte (*Mid Day* (Bombay) 24 February 1993)

The World Bank conducts an independent review of the Sadder Sarovar Project

Baba Amte's main insistence always was that a proper review of the SSP should be made. He was convinced that once people had become aware of all implications of the project the work of building the dam could not possibly go ahead.

Since Baba Amte felt that the Government of Gujarat showed little readiness to enter into dialogue, Baba Amte and other anti-dam activists concentrated their efforts on making the problems involved in this project internationally known.

A first result of their efforts was that Japan, urged by the Japanese branch of the Friends of the Earth Society, cancelled a loan of 25 billion yen which it had promised as help to the SSP.

Next, the President of the World Bank, due to increasing criticism, decided to appoint a commission to conduct an independent review of the Sardar Sarovar Project. Chairman of the commission was Bradford Morse, former administrator of the

United Nations Development Program, Deputy Chairman was Thomas R. Berger, a Canadian, ex-judge and environmentalist.

The Commission started work on September 1, 1991, and handed in its report in June 1992. The commission found that a proper appraisal of the SSP had never been made. When in 1985 the World Bank had approved a loan of 450 million US dollars, it had done so without ascertaining the human and environmental cost of the project.

Regarding rehabilitation the Commission discovered the following facts:

The rehabilitation of two-thirds of the people affected by the project had never even been considered.

Till now only the rehabilitation of people affected by submersion had been taken into consideration. The area of submersion is 38,000 hectares and the number of families affected is about 100,000. But the project also included building a canal bringing water to the drought-prone regions of Saurashtra and the Kutch. This canal which is 450 km long, 250 m wide at the head and 100 m wide at the Rajasthan border, with a distribution network 75,000 km long, will require 80,000 hectares of land, i.e. twice as much as the area of submersion. The people affected by the building of the canal will be twice as many as the people affected by submersion. Yet their rehabilitation had never even been considered.

Regarding the 100.000 people affected by submersion the Commission found that "at least 60 per cent of tribal oustees engaged in cultivating land in Madhya Pradesh and Maharashtra would not get adequate land in resettlement." The reason is this. Tribals cultivated land for generations but never acquired a legally valid title-deed for their land. The States of Maharashtra and Madhya Pradesh decided that only people who hold legally valid title-deeds will have a right to resettlement, the others will be regarded as landless labourers. These tribals told the Commission: "We are not landless labourers, we are farmers."

It should be noted that this treatment of tribals contravenes the Convention 107 passed by the International Labour Organization in 1957 and ratified by India on September

19, 1958. This Convention requires that indigenous and tribal oustees be provided with land of a quality at least equal to the land previously occupied and that the customary usage of land should be respected.

Gujarat has agreed to resettle all oustees, including tribals, on two hectares of land. But only 4,700 oustee families live in Gujarat, 3,000 in Maharashtra and 23,000 in Madhya Pradesh. The Commission also notes: "The fact is that in Madhya Pradesh virtually no steps have been taken towards resettlement and rehabilitation."

Though Gujarat endeavours to provide each oustee family with two hectares of land for resettlement, it should be kept in mind that many oustee families lose much more than 2 hectares. One villager, Mahesh Patel, stands to lose as much as 65 hectares of land due to the impending submergence. To offer to such people two hectares of land for resettlement can hardly be considered a fair compensation (The Independent, March 8, 1993).

As far as the environmental impact of the project is concerned, the Commission stated that since no previous studies on the hydrology of the river and similar subjects had been made, they were not in a position to give definite data. However the data they were able to collect indicate that the impacts upstream and in the command area will be severe.

In conclusion, the commission states that they are fully aware that much money has been spent already on the project, in fact about 2,600 crores of rupees, but that the loss which will be caused by the project is likely to be a multiple of this sum. It states: "A great deal of money has been spent, but we caution that it may be more wasteful to proceed without a full knowledge of the human and environmental cost.... As a result, we think that the wisest course would be for the Bank to step back from the projects and consider them afresh."

The report of the Morse Commission fully corroborates all the objections Baba Amte had brought against the SSP.

The Gujarat Government simply rejected the report of the Morse Commission stating that for them the completion of the SSP was "an article of faith."

India Cancels the WB Loan on Narmada

The current World Bank President, Lewis Preston, accepted the report but decided to continue supporting the SSP. However he laid down conditions which India had to fulfil before March 31, 1993. It soon became evident that India would not be in a position to fulfil these conditions. On March 31, the Bank would have had to declare that it suspended further payment. To spare the World Bank the need of giving reasons for suspending payment, India on March 30 cancelled the World Bank loan on Narmada. This means India rejected the 170 million dollars of the loan of 450 million dollars which the WB had made to India in 1985. The rest of that loan had already been used up. And India withdrew the application it had made for a loan of 350 million dollars to complete the canal and the application for 90 million dollars for the Narmada Basin Development Project. Many people felt that cancelling the loan was a face-saving device.

The Consequences of Cancelling the WB Loan

In an article in the *Times of India* April 2, 1993 entitled 'Doubts persist over founding Narmada', Ashrad Sayed carefully examines the possibility of completing the SSP without help from the WB, and he concludes; "It is now feared that the project is bound to be delayed on account of paucity of funds and it may become a white elephant to the people of Gujarat."

The Question of Lowering the Height of the Dam

The Chief Minister of Madhya Pradesh, in a letter to the Prime Minister, had pleaded that the height of the dam be lowered from 455 feet to 436 feet. He pointed out that by thus lowering the height of the dam the water supply to Gujarat would not suffer any loss, but 67 villages in Madhya Pradesh would be saved from immersion. It would lessen the burden of rehabilitation on Madhya Pradesh, since 36,000 families less would have to be rehabilitated. Also the Narmada Water Dispute Tribunal declared that the height of 436 feet would assure the required capacity of the reservoir, i.e. 6.18 million acre-feet of water.

Gujarat declared that the height of the dam was 'not negotiable'. Gujarat felt that though the lowering of the dam would not diminish the water required for irrigation it would affect the generation of power. This would seem to indicate that Gujarat's main concern was the generation of power. Also the Morse Commission had been struck by Gujarat's lack of interest in supplying water to the people in the drought-prone areas. They write: "We were surprised that the plans for the delivery of water to the people in the drought-prone regions in Gujarat were only in the earliest stages of development."

NGOs in Gujarat are also unhappy over the measly share of water for the drought-prone areas in Saurashtra (9.5 per cent) and the Kutch (1.5 per cent). They want legislation to stop the use of water in northern Gujarat where rich farmers with political clout are said to be programming Narmada water for 10 new sugar factories. The NGOs say: "We shall not be party to the Kulaks cornering the gains."

Gujarat's lack of interest to supply water to the drought-prone areas and the withdrawal of an application to the WB for a loan of 350 million dollars to complete the canal, give additional poignancy to an apprehension of Baba Amte: "It is more than likely that there will be no money left to build the branch canals of the SSP. Without these canals no one in Saurashtra and Kutch will get even a drop of water from the SSP (*Cry, the Beloved Narmada*, p. 9).

SSP-hit Families Vow not to Budge

Baba Amte had organized a door-to-door referendum in 230 out of the 245 villages in the submergence zone of the SSP. Each adult family member was asked whether she or he was prepared to leave their home and land. More than 22,000 people voted that they would not move from their village or home come rain or flood. This has been described as the first major people's struggle since independence. The result of this referendum was declared by Baba Amte on March 1993 in a meeting held under the massive Rajghat Bridge which is expected to be submerged in the next five years. Present at the meeting were Medha Patkar, Mrinal Gore, B.D. Sharma, former Commissioner for Scheduled

Castes and Tribes, Sadanand Varde, former Maharashtra Minister for Education, Count Tarnowski, London, an Italian television crew, many other important people and 3,000 tribals.

Baba Amte, along with all those affected by the Narmada project, took a pledge that they would not leave their home, land or village. "We will drown but not move."

The land which the tribals had cultivated for generations was not considered to be their land. They were treated as landless labourers. All they had to look forward to was a life in the slums without any source of income. They preferred to die on the land they regarded as their own in protest against the injustice done to them.

Baba was determined to live up to the pledge he had taken. He often spoke of his body floating on the waters of the Narmada. In 1994 when the flood waters of the Narmada reached his hut, he decided to remain, but the Collector with a number of officials came, physically lifted him and took him to the Badwani Government rest house.

What did Baba Amte achieve by staying at the Narmada?

His first intention was to give comfort and strength to the tribals in the Narmada valley by becoming one with them and thus assuring them that they were not altogether forgotten and forsaken. This he has most certainly achieved.

He wanted to make sure that the people ousted from the valley get a decent rehabilitation. This was not quite without success.

In the past when high dams have been built, people living in the submerged area have often been evicted without proper compensation. Compensation in such cases, did not usually include anything more than cash, and the cash was rarely if ever sufficient to buy replacement land. Even the SSP in the beginning paid little attention to rehabilitation. When in 1960/61 the land of six villages were expropriated to establish the construction site of the dam, no thought was given to resettlement and the 50,000 inhabitants of the six villages were driven from their homes with nowhere to go. Later, under pressure exerted by Baba Amte, Medha Patkar and many others, more attention was paid to resettlement. Though even now rehabilitation is less than perfect, the oustees of the SSP are better looked after than the oustees of any other project. When leaving Anandwan for Narmada Baba Amte said: "Now when the sun of my life is about to set, I have set out to catch the rising sun of environmental awareness." There can be no doubt that Baba Amte's stay at the Narmada river has contributed much to awaken environmental awareness both in India and abroad.

Baba Amte is convinced that the development policy of the future is being decided at the Narmada. The Narmada did, indeed become the area of a struggle for a society "in which there must be sufficiency for all before there is superfluity for some."

Patrick McCully states, regarding the cancelling of the World Bank loan: "For the Bank to have to get out of the project after eight years of active support is a humiliating defeat with wide-ranging implication for the Bank and the mega projects it supports around the world" (*Illustrated Weekly of India*, May 8-14, 1993, p 10). There will be greater attention paid to protecting nature and there will be a greater readiness to work for the abolition of poverty rather than to help the rich becoming richer.

Baba Amte was not wrong in anticipating that "My presence at the Narmada river will be enough. The sound of my silence will be enough to help people to hear the cry of the Narmada."

8

Sources of Baba Amte's Spirituality

When asked whether he had drawn inspiration from any particular school of thought or leader Amte replied: "Yes, from several: Marx, Ruskin, Mao, Kropotkin, Tagore and Gandhi."

The fact that he mentioned Kropotkin indicates that he does not merely mention names without having read their books. Kropotkin is hardly ever mentioned nowadays, though in his own time Prince Peter Kropotkin (1842-1921) was a famous and influential writer. His *Memoirs of a Revolutionist* has been translated into all major languages and his book: *Mutual Aid, a Factor of Evolution* is a much needed corrective not only to the opinion that class-war is the main dynamic element of social revolution, but also to Darwin's theory of 'the survival of the fittest'. Amte certainly found Kropotkin's writing appealing, and 'mutual aid' is an important factor in Amte's notion of a creative revolution.

Whatever inspiration Amte may have derived from the great thoughts of Marx and Mao, Marxist revolution, as it was actually carried out, did not appeal to him, neither did he admire Mao's Cultural Revolution. When he was writing he had not yet seen how the East European nations threw off the oppressive and enslaving yoke of communism, but he mentions that the workers' government had to hide its face when Solidarity gained an overwhelming victory.

Quite different was his relationship with Tagore and Gandhi. He not only read their writings but knew them personally and was intimately acquainted with them. He writes: "I could live in the company of two universal souls that inhabited Shantiniketan (Tagore's university) and Sevagram (Gandhi's ashram at Wardha). I quarrelled with both of them, loved them immensely and also earned their love."

Tagore's Influence

During his student years Murlidhar travelled to Calcutta and was staying at Shantiniketan because he had fallen in love with Tagore's music.

Rabindranath Tagore had grown up in the tradition of the Brahmo Samaj, the spiritual movement started by Raja Ram Mohan Roy. Ram Mohan Roy, who is acknowledged as the Father of modern India, was convinced that India needs a strong spiritual foundation if she is to achieve real greatness and prosperity and that the worship of the one true God in spirit and truth was this foundation.

Rabindranath's father, Devendranath Tagore, who succeeded Ram Mohan Roy as leader of the Brahmo Samaj, thus formulated the basic tenet of the Samaj:

The Supreme Being alone was in the beginning; nothing else existed. He created the universe. He is eternal, infinite, all-wise, all merciful, independent, formless and one without a second, all-pervading, ruling-all, all-containing, all-knowing, all-powerful, the permanent, the perfect, the one beyond all-comparison. In His worship alone lies our welfare in this world and in the world to come. To love Him and to do the works He loves is His worship.

To love him and to do the works he loves means to follow the law, the Sanatana Dharma, which God has imprinted in man's mind, the law which finds expression in the voice of conscience.

Fearlessly obeying the law of conscience the Brahmos carried on a relentless fight against all the evils which had crept into the Indian tradition. They fought against sati, the worship of the many gods, against monism, caste discrimination and similar evils.

The Brahmos consider God to be both immanent and transcendent. They did not identify themselves with God, but see God residing and working in all things. As a great Brahmo expressed it:

The Divine Spirit permeates every pore of matter and humanity, and yet is absolutely different from both. There is no flight of fowls to their evening home that is not directed by the unerring hand of Divine Love. There is no lily in the field nor rose in the valley whose blossom and fragrance do not come from the breath of infinite beauty. There is no beauty, no wisdom, no faithfulness, no purity, no piety and self-sacrifice that is not inspired by Him. The goodness of all the good is a ray of reflection from Him, the greatness of all the great points to His throne on high." (P.C. Mozoomdar, *The Oriental Christ*, p. 41).

Striving after perfection is striving for an ever greater love of God, it is striving to be one with God who dwells in men and in nature. Tagore's poems are the most delicate expression of this love of God. They are just a commentary on verses of the *Isa Upanishad*:

"All this, whatever moves on earth, is pervaded by the Lord. Renounce it first and then be filled with joy. Covet not the goods of anyone at all" (*Isa Upanishad* 1.1).

In order to foster this way of life Rabindranath Tagore founded Shantiniketan, a school situated in the most beautiful natural surroundings. By turning serious work into joyful play Tagore managed to create a community united in joy, work and love. For Tagore, Shantiniketan was a microcosm of the world as he had wished it to be.

It is not difficult to see the influence of Tagore in the Anandwan established by Baba Amte; in the way in which Amte made himself one with the leprosy patients and in the spirit of joy by which Anandwan lives up to its name.

The Inspiration from Mahatma Gandhi's Life and Teaching

"Most religious men I have met," says Gandhiji, "are politicians in disguise. I however, who wear the guise of a politician, am at heart a religious man" He tells us: "My religion is based on Truth and Non-violence. Truth is my God, and Non-Violence the means to reach Him."

"God is that undefinable something which we all feel but which we do not know. To me, God is truth and love, God is ethics and morality, God is fearlessness. God is the source of light and life, and yet he is above and beyond all these. God is conscience." (*Young India*, 5-8-1925).

The particular image under which Gandhiji chooses to worship God is Truth. In later years he does no longer say that God is Truth, but rather, that Truth is God. Gandhiji is not so much a theorist as a man of action. He prefers to define God in terms of a practical method of approaching Him rather than in terms of an abstract idea. We experience God by experiencing what is best in us. This may seem strange to some people, but it is not strange to people who follow the teaching of the Bhagavad Gita. There God declares:

In water I am the flavour,
In sun and moon the light,
In all the Vedas Om,
In space I am sound: in man his manliness and I,
Pure fragrance in the earth am I,
Flame's onset in the fire:
and life am I in all contingent beings:
In ascetics their fierce austerity,
Know that I am the eternal seed
Of all contingent beings;
Reason in the rational,
Glory in the glorious am I,
Power in the powerful I,
Such power as knows not passion nor desire:
Desire am I in contingent beings,
But such desire as is not at war with righteousness.
(*Bhagavad Gita,* 7:8-11).

Clinging to the Truth

By saying Truth is God, Gandhiji intends to state that we can approach God by clinging to the Truth, by being true to what is best in us. Clinging to the Truth means being faithful to the voice within, to the voice of conscience, to the voice of God.

Clinging to God, therefore, means clinging to the *sanatana dharma,* clinging to the law which is imprinted in man's heart. Clinging to the *sanatana dharma* is not necessarily the same as clinging to the written *dharma,* the traditional law. The *sanatana dharma* is higher than all traditional or written law.

It is an ancient Indian insight that on account of human

weakness errors may creep into the traditional law. From time to time people with deep spiritual insight will discover such errors and condemn them in the light of their insight into the *sanatana dharma.*

The Kshatriya *dharma* is considered to be the sacred law binding on all warriors. Yet Yudhishthira, the king of Righteousness, condemns the Kshatriya *dharma* in the most scathing terms because it has led to senseless slaughter (*Mahabharata,* 12:7:5).

R.C. Zaehner, in his book *Hinduism* rightly gives to the chapter on Tagore, Gandhi, and the other reformers, the title: 'Yudhishthira Returns'. Though orthodox Hindus maintain that untouchability is prescribed by the Hindu *dharma,* and the law of Manu seems to bear them out, the reformers agree with Gandhiji, who following in the footsteps of Yudhishthira declares. "I decline to be bound by any interpretation of *dharma,* however learned it may be, if it is repugnant to reason and to moral sense," and he declared untouchability to be an ineffaceable blot which Hinduism carries with it", and insisted that it be abolished.

Ahimsa

To be faithful to God, in the mind of Gandhiji, means to be faithful to the voice of conscience, which is the voice of God. "The way to God," he says, "is ahimsa, non-violence." What does he mean by ahimsa?

In the sense of non-killing ahimsa has long been a part of the Hindu-Jain tradition of Gandhiji's native Gujarat. But in Gandhi's mind the word ahimsa has taken on a deeper and more extensive meaning. Negatively, it now means "avoiding injury to anything on earth in thought, word and deed." Positively, it is "not merely a state of harmlessness, but a positive state of love, of doing good even to the evil-doer."

"Literally speaking, ahimsa means non-killing. But to me it has a world of meaning and takes me into a world much higher, infinitely higher, than the realm to which I would go, if I merely understood by ahimsa non-killing. Ahimsa really means that you may not offend anybody; you may not harbour any uncharitable thought even in connection with one who may consider himself to be your enemy.... If we return blow for blow, we depart from the doctrine of ahimsa. But I go further. If we resent a friend's action or the so-called enemy's action, we still fall short of this doctrine. But when I say, we should not resent, I do not say that we should acquiesce: but by resenting I mean wishing that some harm should be done to the enemy, or that he should be put out of the way, not even by any action of ours, but by the action of somebody else, or say, Divine Agency. If we harbour even this thought we depart from the doctrine of ahimsa" (Address to the Y.M,C.A. Madras 16.2.1916).

Gandhiji makes a sharp distinction between 'the ahimsa of the weak' and the ahimsa of the strong.' He wants to have nothing to do with the ahimsa of weak which is mere cowardice and failure to protect the weak. When some villagers had fled from a tiger instead of protecting their wives and children and then boasted of being followers of ahimsa, he publicly called them cowards and praised the courage of those who had shot the tiger. By ahimsa he meant the courage to stand up against violence and injustice unarmed. Ahimsa, thus understood, was for him the only legitimate and effective weapon a man can use against injustice and evil.

"Non-Violence is the greatest force at the disposal of mankind. It is the law of our species as violence is the law of the brute."

The Mahatma is convinced that Satyagraha, if it is genuinely non-violent, will be infallibly effective. Man is a spirit; there is a divine spark in him. Hence even the oppressed masses can be trained to the superhuman courage and love which satyagraha demands. They merely have to be aroused to the awareness of their true dignity. And the oppressors, no matter how ruthless and violent they are, will never be quite beyond the reach of suffering love. "The hardest heart and the grossest ignorance must disappear before the force of suffering without anger and malice".

Though the Mahatma became the centre and leader of India's massive movement for independence, he never saw himself primarily as a political leader. The central idea of his life was a search for God, a search for God-realization through self-realization.

The liberation of India which he had in mind was not merely a liberation from foreign domination: it was a liberation of the whole man: freedom from egoistic passions, freedom from hate, anger, avarice, sloth, a liberation from the slavery to what Indian tradition calls the six enemies of man: *Kamam* (lust), *Krodham* (anger), *lobham* (greed), *moham* (avarice), *ahamkaram* (pride) and *alasyam* (sloth). The struggle for liberation, in the Mahatma's mind, was a struggle for the freedom from sin, not merely a freedom from the British. The fight for national independence was incidental to the main struggle which for him was the struggle for the recovery of India's dignity, self-respect and soul.

The first step in a creative revolution is to awaken man to an awareness of the divine qualities inherent in him, the awareness of having been created in the image of God, an awareness coupled with the determination to be true to oneself. Our actions must agree with what is best in us, they must bear witness to the truth in us:

"That our actions must be in agreement with our being is not the last, but the first step of practical religion. Without this foundation it is impossible to build up the practice of religion."

It is with reference to this endeavour of awakening man to the awareness of this true dignity that Amte said:

"There is no substitute to Gandhi's endeavour of rousing the impoverished masses to creative awareness." While the ultimate goal is the achievement of Moksha, the immediate temporal goal for which Gandhiji was striving, was swaraj or Ramraj, conceived not merely as political independence but as a complete social revolution. The India of his dreams was a community of self-governing, self-sufficient villages, each administered by largely autonomous, elected panchayats and supporting itself in frugal sufficiency through co-operative agriculture and cottage industries. Decentralization, both political and economic, is the key-word in Gandhian planning. He is strongly opposed to a highly centralised, powerful state, which he sees as a continual threat to the freedom and growth of the individual. Ideally the state should wither away giving place to an enlightened anarchy where every one is his own ruler. He rules himself in such a manner, that he is never a hindrance to his neighbour." In Gandhiji's mind the individual is the one supreme consideration.

Gandhiji's concept of private property is contained in his well-known principle of 'Trusteeship'. The owner has the right to what he needs for his subsistence, but the surplus must be regarded as a trust, which he holds from God on behalf of the needy. Baba Amte has been called the last true Gandhian. This is not how he sees himself. He willingly acknowledges having received inspiration from many quarters. But he is not anyone's follower. He is an independent thinker and is bent on going his own way. His supreme law is to be true to himself. He says: "I think we should avoid tutelage to any dogma or to any leader, past or present."

Inspiration from Sane Guruji

The public figure with whom Amte felt most one in mind and heart was Sane Guruji. Out of the 90 pages of Amte's last book *Karunecha Kalam* eleven pages are devoted to his memory. Sane Guruji was a warm-hearted man, he loved children and flowers, he felt one with all that was beautiful in nature, he felt one with all the people who were suffering and oppressed and he had a glowing love for India, his motherland. He had inherited his warm-heartedness from his mother, a woman who had never gone to school, who could neither read nor write and yet was endowed with sublime wisdom and a most refined culture.

Sane Guruji says: "My mother taught me to speak to people with love. She not only taught me to love my fellow-beings but she also taught me to love the nature around me—birds and beasts in the fields, trees and flowers."

So complete was her influence on her son, so much love did she shower on him, that in later life all objects of love and veneration appear to him in the form of a mother. His country became his beloved motherland and he loved the whole world because it was the manifestation and offspring of the Mother of the Universe. He could think of God only as mother.

Sane Guruji has written many books, but the one book which has captured the hearts of the whole Marathi-speaking world, a book which has gone through many reprints and is found on the bookshelf of every Marathi household, is *Shyamchi Aai* (The Mother of Shyam) in which he describes his own mother. At the end of this book Shyam says: "Friends, this was my mother. It is a great fortune to get a mother like this in this world. All that is good, all that is holy in me is a gift of my mother. She died, but before she died she taught me how to serve my motherland."

When the freedom struggle began Sane Guruji enthusiastically joined in the satyagraha movement and like thousands of other satyagrahis landed in jail. He was transferred to a jail in Trichy. There he was together with satyagrahis from all over India. There it struck him how little they knew of one another. They did not know the language of other states, much less did they know their literature and culture. Thus he began to dream of Antar-Bharati, an institution where teachers and students from all states would get together and hear and learn the different languages of the country; books from one language would be translated into others and everyone would come to know India's common culture in all its variety.

As Rabindranath Tagore's Vishwa Bharati became the great centre of World learning, Antar Bharati was meant to be a place where people could become familiar with India's great national heritage. Antar Bharati would thus become the fountainhead of that new India which was about to be born. Antar Bharati was the slogan which Amte proclaimed in the *Shram shibirs* at Somnath and inspired his 'Knit-India' marches.

After India had become independent and the Congress had become a ruling party, Sane Guruji was deeply pained seeing the power struggle, the selfishness and corruption that went along with it. Amte joined the Socialist Party hoping that it would be a movement for the uplift of the whole country and would pay special attention to the poor and oppressed. Sane Guruji's vision of a new India was very similar to that of Baba Amte. He wrote:

"I want to see India free of hatred and full of friendship where people live in happy comradeship. I want to see my countrymen learning different languages, studying other cultures, growing in knowledge, cultivating the arts, striving to bring about a just social order and maintaining at the same time the dignity of personal freedom.

"In the country of my dream there are no touchables and untouchables; the cities are crowded with busy people, industries are nationalized, people are busy providing for their immediate needs and marching forward. Various new experiments are carried out in its laboratories, there is no ignorance, no disease, no hide¬bound customs; young people are climbing the heights of the Himalayas and diving into the deep sea or making friends with death like Nachiketa in search of knowledge.

"Let our eyes see this country steeped in scientific knowledge and pursuing a great ideal, for after all, it is your dreams and your desires which will shape the future of this country" (R.M. Gole: *Sane Guruji, the Man and His Mission,* p. 49-50).

Sane Guruji was not an idle dreamer but a fighter. He was shocked when he found that even the great temple of Pandharpur was not open to Harijans. Varkaris did not observe caste distinction during their pilgrimage. Yet when they reached Pandharpur only the high caste people were allowed to enter the temple, Harijans were prohibited. Sane Guruji announced his intention to go on a fast unto death unless the Pandharpur temple was thrown open to Harijans. Some friends persuaded him to wait for six months during which time they would try to achieve this through a high pressure public campaign. In 1947 a whirlwind campaign against untouchability roused people into action. A committee under Maharshi Karve was appointed to find a way out. The temple priests came with tomes of religious works to argue their case.

Guruji silenced them saying that one need not seek religious sanction to treat each and every human being as a human being. Since the movement failed Sane Guruji began his fast unto death. The news of his fast spread far and wide. There was great excitement. Some people advised him to give up the fast. Government offered to intervene. Some condemned it as an act of violence. The climax of this dramatic incident was reached, when in a telegram, Gandhiji informed Sane Guruji that, in his opinion, the fast was ill-conceived and should be given up. In a respectful letter Sane Guruji informed Gandhiji that his resolve was irrevocable. In his letter he said:

"In my speeches I have told thousands of my listeners that if the Pandharpur temple was not thrown open to the Harijans on the eleventh day of the bright half of Vaishakh I would fast unto death. They heard me with tears in their eyes. What I told them was not just a platform gimmick but my most sincere resolve. If I don't live up to it now, it will be their deception and my life will become meaningless because I shall have lost something which I hold very near and dear and value most in myself.

"You will understand how with a very sad heart I am writing this to you. But have you not taught us that there comes a moment in man's life when, if the whole world goes against him, he must remain true to his convictions" (R.M. Gole: *Sane Guruji, the Man and His Mission,* p. 63).

Finally the resistance of the priests was gradually worn down and the Pandharpur temple was thrown open to Harijans. There was a tremendous rejoicing throughout the country.

Sane Guruji shared Amte's admiration for the common people, particularly he was wondering where his mother, an illiterate woman, got her refined culture from. Gradually he came to the conclusion that the popular stories which mothers tell their children and the songs which women sing when grinding the corn and harvesting the fields were the stream that carried the most precious cultural wealth from generation to generation, stories and songs which often have a very deep meaning.

He went from village to village collecting these simple traditional folk-songs. He used every stratagem to remove the shyness of the simple women in order to learn the songs. He would help them in their daily chores, sit with them at the grinding stone, clean or cut vegetables with them, draw water from the well. Soon he was accepted as a welcome guest everywhere he went and songs began to pour from the lips of the women he met. He was all ears while they sang and took care to note down every song he heard. He collected nearly 2000 of these popular songs, sorted them out subject-wise and wrote detailed appreciations of them all. When published in book form they were an instant success.

Amte gives his chapter on Sane Guruji the title: A Record of Tears.

"Since God himself cannot be present everywhere, he created the mother to spread the grace and fragrance of true love. In order to strengthen the resolve to carry this love beyond the fence of one's own home, God created a great human being with the heart of a mother: Pandurang Sadashiv Sane." Asian tradition has perceived since ancient times that there is more life and force in things which are tender and soft than in things which are hardened and strong.

"Soft and tender man is born,
Hardened and strong he dies,
Stiff and unbending are the ways of death
Tender and wayward the ways of life
There is nothing softer and more yielding in the world than water,
But nothing has more strength also to bend what is strong and stiff.
All the world knows: What is weak defeats what is strong
What is soft defeats things that are stiff..."
Thus Lao-Tzu states in the sixty-seventh and eightieth sayings.
Sane Guruji proclaims this great truth in the words
"Through my tears I shall reach my ideal;
In my tears rests the power to crush steel and stone.
My tears are my God.
Never deprive me of my tears
Let my eyelids never get dry."

(Karunecha Kalam p. 33).

Baba Amte shares Sane Guruji's conviction that much of what is beautiful and of value in life owes its growth to tears of compassion, to kinship in pain (*Karunecha Kalam* pp. 32-42).

9

Baba Amte's Spiritual Journey

When Baba Amte was asked what name could be given to the philosophy that guides him, he replied: "If you must put a label to what guides my action, it would be 'creative humanism'. Humanism is the philosophy which puts man in the centre and considers man's development as the main concern that should guide all our actions. Baba Amte is in fact, widely acknowledged as a great humanist. When the G.D. Birla Foundation established an International Award for Outstanding Contribution to Humanism, Baba Amte was the first person to whom this award was given. In the Citation it is stated:

"The G.D. Birla International Award for outstanding Contribution to Humanism has been instituted by the Birla Academy for Arts and Culture to foster the universal humanist vision enshrined in our country's Vedic tradition and upheld by the great sons of India. We are happy that the first award goes to Baba Amte, an exemplary practitioner of creative humanism in its myriad aspects...."

On the occasion of the fortieth anniversary of the adoption of the Universal Declaration of Human Rights by the United Nations six persons, chosen from among all the nations, were honoured with awards for outstanding achievements in the field of human rights. Baba Amte was one of the six. The Human Rights Declaration was adopted by the General Assembly of the U.N. on Dec. 10, 1948. The formal ceremony for the award of the prizes took place in the General Assembly Hall in New York on 8th December 1988 Danta M. Caputo, President of the General Assembly, said: "Baba Amte, an indefatigable warrior for the poor, the handicapped, the underprivileged is most meritorious of the honour from the United Nations." (UN & On Newsletter, 17 December 1988).

Even earlier Baba Amte was in many ways honoured and acknowledged as a great humanist: He received the Padmashri.

(1971) the Rashtra Bhushan 1978, the Damien Dutton Award (1983), the Magsaysay Award (1985).

Humanistic movements in Europe during the last centuries were to a large extent atheistic movements. Their promoters thought man could achieve real freedom only when he denies any dependence on God.

Amte's creative humanism is not of that type. The Birla Academy gave its first award to Baba Amte for "fostering the universal humanist vision enshrined in our country's Vedic tradition and upheld by the great sons of India." In the Vedic tradition of India man's greatness consists in being a reflection and expression of the splendour of the Infinite Being which upholds this visible universe.

Ramanujacharya, the great Indian sage, thus describes the Infinite Being: "His divine form is the depository of all radiance, loveliness, fragrance, beauty and youth – desirable, congruous, uniform, unthinkable, divine, marvellous, eternal, indefectible, perfect. His essence and nature are not to be limited by word or thought. He is an ocean of boundless compassion, moral excellence, tenderness, generosity and sovereignty, refuge of the whole world, without distinction of persons. The one ocean of tenderness to all who resort to Him. He takes away the sorrows of his devotees and becomes incarnate simply out of compassion, to give light to the whole world with his indefectible and perfect glory, and to fill all things with his loveliness." (Ramanuja: *Commentary on the Bhagavad Gita* 6:47)

By deriving his existence from the Infinite Being man also has a share in its splendour and beauty. By an increasing awareness of being rooted in the Infinite Being man builds up in himself a sense of dignity and self-esteem. Man's behaviour is determined by his self-awareness. His behaviour must be in keeping with his being. Man must be true to himself. An improved self-awareness is bound to create and release in man new energies which lead to a determined attempt not only at self-improvement but also at trying to make the world a better place to live in. Amte, therefore, rightly calls his spiritual attitude 'creative humanism.'

Baba Amte sees the essence of religion neither in performing rituals and ceremonies, nor in wearing saffron-coloured robes nor in visiting temples, but in doing God's will. He says: "Work is worship; work is my religion for work builds." This is also the way in which the Brahmo Samaj looks at divine worship. Already Devendranath Tagore had stated: "To love God and to do the works he loves is his worship."

The Templeton Award is an award given 'for progress in religion.' Baba Amte rightly assumed that by giving this award to him the Templeton Foundation approved of his notion of religion.

'In his reply to the Templeton Foundation Baba Amte states: For me there is no better religion than the one that builds inside human beings a sense of dignity and self-esteem. I am glad that this definition of religion seems acceptable. I am not religious, traditionally speaking, but I feel religion is that force which builds a stronger and more righteous human being."

The Templeton Foundation's criteria of choosing a person for the reward appear to approve of Amte's notion of religion. The criteria are that the work of the nominee must result in a deeper spiritual awareness on the part of man, a better understanding of life, a heightened quality of devotion and love which will release new and creative energies into human society today (The *Hitvada,* Thursday, March 8, 1990). The Templeton Award was established in 1972 by financier John Templeton, a Presbyterian, who keeps the amount higher than the Nobel prizes in the belief that religion is more important. Previous winners have included Mother Teresa, Evangelist Billy Graham, the Soviet writer Alexander Solzehnitsyn.

Baba Amte's Spiritual Journey

The specific feature of Baba Amte's spiritual journey is that he starts with a quest for human values and that this very quest leads him to a greater knowledge and love of God. In his early years Baba Amte felt that warm human life could be found in the company of the common people rather than in the society of the wealthy elite. He came to admire 'the richness of heart among the poor people' which compared favourably with "the poverty of heart of the rich." He, therefore, renounced his wealth and became one with the common people, because he found: "the common man, he is the uncommon man." He felt that there was a divine quality in the greatness of the common people. Referring to tribals and to simple farmers Amte said: "It was after seeing the greatness of people like these that 1 became convinced that God is always there in their hearts, sleeping like a baby."

Creative humanism, as Amte sees it, consists in making people aware of the god-like qualities which God has implanted in their hearts, or to use Baba's own words: "It consists in awakening God who is always there in their hearts, sleeping like a baby." It was this quest for creative humanism which led Baba Amte to renounce his wealth in order to become one with the common people.

Freedom from the slavery to respectability gave to Baba also a greater freedom in his attitude to God: He said, "After murmuring 'Your Honour', 'Your Lordship' to magistrates for all these years, I started shouting 'Your Lordship' to the real God."

Baba's resolve to consecrate his life to the service of leprosy patients was likewise based on humanistic rather than religious motives. When he had left Tulshiram, the dying leprosy patient, lying in the rain because of the fear which had gripped him, he could no longer look on himself as a fearless person; his self-image had been shattered. He says: "I am upset, I am very much disappointed when I see within me a wrong image of myself" (*Ujjwal Udyasathi,* p. 24). It was clear to him: If he did not banish this fear he could not have any self-respect any more. He would have lost that self-image which alone makes life worth living. He took up leprosy work to overcome that fear in his life. But since being true to oneself means being true to God, his resolve to build a friendship with his suffering brothers and sisters ultimately was a religious decision.

Amte felt as much when he said: "When there is fear, there is no love, where there is no love there is no God."

For both Rabindranath Tagore and Mahatma Gandhi, God reveals himself in the voice of our conscience. Baba had learned from these great masters to consider God as the light which makes us see the path we have to follow.

God is Love

A time came when Amte began to realize that God not only gives light, but also gives us strength to follow the light; that God not only points the way but also helps us to go the way he points out. He had a strong sense of God's helping hand, when they struck water, abundant water in the well they were digging in a dry stretch of land, at Anandwan. He recalls, "We worshipped the water with white flowers and milk. Then for the rest of the day we sat by our well just staring delighted at the water. Now we had reason to look hopefully into the future."

Still more intensely did he feel the nearness of God's helping love when an international group of students happened to come to Anandwan and built a dispensary and other buildings just when they were needed to make sure that Anandwan would not remain merely a farm but would be a place where leprosy patients were properly cared for.

Having thus experienced God's loving care, Amte resolved never to refuse anyone who came to Anandwan for help, be he or she blind or lame or otherwise disabled; never to ask whether there was enough grain or money or accommodation, but to accept people trusting in God's help, Amte expresses his conviction in the words: "Wherever God has pointed the way with His finger, he has also cleared the way with His mighty palm."

Some Characteristics of Amte's Religious Outlook

In an interview with Fortune, a quarterly published by the UNICEF Regional Office, New Delhi, Amte gives us an insight into some characteristics of his spiritual outlook.

Faith in God should be free from all Taint of Communalism

In this interview Amte says: "A man of faith is not necessarily a Hindu or Muslim or Christian." Faith in God, as

Amte understands it, must be free from all taint of communalism. In India, stress on religious conviction, not rarely leads to communal strife. This happens when communal interests get mixed up with religion. Genuine faith in God does not divide but unites. True believers are aware that God is one. He is the common Father of us all. Genuine faith in God leads all people, to whatever community, race or caste they may belong, to regard and love one another as God's dear children.

It is Amte's firm conviction: "A religion which is not able to unite people with one another, will also not be able to unite people with God." Amte is careful not to do anything that would mark his establishment as a Hindu institution. There is no temple in Anandwan, no picture of any deity, no formal prayers. This has misled a writer to state: "Amte does not believe that God is the creator and controller of the universe. There is no need in asking for God's help..." When this was pointed out to Amte, he shook his head and said: "How can they say such a thing, when I repeat over and over again: "whenever God points the way with his finger he also clears the way with His mighty, palm."

On his 'Knit-India' tour he was asked to inaugurate a leprosy clinic which had been named: 'Shri Ram Seva Tirth'. He asked the officer in charge to remove the name 'Shri Ram' and proceeded to inaugurate the clinic.

Faith is not Other-Worldly

Many people think that a man bent on spiritual progress should renounce all interest in earthly affairs. Lokmanya Tilak tells us that the people among whom he was growing up held this view. He found this most distressing. He not only had a desire for a deeply spiritual life, but was also bent on serving his country. The idea that these two ideals were mutually exclusive was to him unbearable, as he wanted to pursue both.

In order to find a way out of this difficulty he started a careful study of the Bhagavad Gita. To his great joy he found that far from regarding these two ideals as mutually exclusive, the Gita taught that they complete one another: that true spirituality is the strongest motive for service, that love of God must prove itself in the service done to society. In his famous book, Gita

Rahasya Tilak interprets Karma Yoga as service done to society (N.G. Jog: *Bal Gangadhar Tilak,* Delhi 1962, p. 196-199).

Baba Amte reached the same conclusion. He says: "Spirituality is not otherworldly. Science and spirituality are two sides of the same coin. An introspective search for order in an indi¬vidual and the universe is spirituality. When that search is turned outward we call it Science. Both spirituality and science are to be applied to transform human condition." (UNICEF Report p. 10)

The Inward Way

By calling spirituality an 'introspective search' Amte follows the classical path of India's spirituality: the inward way. It is the way which has been pointed out already in the Katha Upanishad:

"A certain sage in search of immortality.
Turned his eyes inward and he saw the self within" (4:1).

By entering into ourselves we become aware of expectations which are inseparable from our innermost self; expectations which arise from the very centre of our being. We find that our hearts are set on total security, on a love that lasts, on unclouded happiness. To believe in God means to believe in ourselves: We believe that what is best in us, our most noble desires, are not doomed to frustration but are capable of fulfilment. We believe that our desire for *satyam, shivam, sundaram* will find its fulfilment in Him who is *sacchidananda.*

Just as faith in God is the expression of a positive attitude to life, and thus reveals a healthy mind, atheism involves an attitude of despair; it is the expression of a sickly mind. By denying the existence of God we resign ourselves to be doomed to frustration.

Friedrich Nietzsche, the philosopher who proclaimed God is dead, vividly experienced what it means to be an atheist. He writes:

"You will never pray any more, never adore, never take rest in infinite trust – you renounce standing still before an infinite wisdom, ultimate goodness, ultimate power and let your thoughts take rest – You have no abiding guardian and friend in your seven fold loneliness – you live without having the view on a mountain which has snow on its summit and fire in its heart – for you there is none to reward, none to add the last touch of perfection – there is no reason any more in all that happens, no love in all that will befall you – there is no resting place any more for your heart – man of renunciation, in all that you will renounce, who will give you the strength for it? No one ever had such strength!" (Froehliche Wissenschaft, n. 385).

Finding God in Science

Amte says: "Spirituality and science are two sides of the same coin." Science for a man of faith is merely an attempt at rethinking the thoughts of God which are incorporated in the structure of nature. When Kepler, the great astronomer, had succeeded in formulating the laws by which planets move, he said the beautiful prayer: "These are your thoughts, O God, I merely endeavour to rethink them."

God has made man the king and ruler of the universe. Scientific research is rethinking God's thoughts in order to make our life healthier, richer and more beautiful. Amte vigorously studied science to find better means of curing leprosy patients, of making fields yield richer crops, of preserving nature; he studied social science in order to promote cooperation for the common good.

Finding God in His Image

One could describe Amte's life as a search for God, as an increasing awareness of God, God not understood as a postulate of practical reason but God as he manifests Himself in the godlike qualities of our own being. Gandhiji already said: "God is fearlessness." Also in Amte's self-esteem the awareness of his fearlessness played an important part. He was, therefore, extremely upset when he was aware of having yielded to fear by running away and not coming to the aid of Tulshiram, the dying leprosy patient, lying deserted in the rain, and he did everything to overcome that fear in his life.

To be true to onself, for a man of faith, also means to acknowledge God as the source of all that is good and noble in us. All that is good in us is only the reflection of some aspect of God's own perfection.

We are only an image of God. We cannot boast about the god- like qualities in our being as if we had given them to ourselves, but we must thank God and give credit to God for all the good which we have or do.

The real test of spiritual greatness is humility; it is the recognition that we have to carry on a constant fight against a trend to vanity. Baba Amte has this mark of greatness in a high degree. He confesses: "I also have a chronic temptation to vanity - my ego feels very nice when someone gives it a message, but I know it is numbing, not curing. I pray daily for success and defeat. I crave for both equally because the ebb and flow make you scale new heights.... You have to strip yourself of your vanity, your pride and the blistering ulcers of dishonesty. It requires great courage to face one's own self, but in all these things honesty and courage are twins (Graham Turner, *More than Conquerors* pp. 187-188).

Amte's ideal is 'to be a man for others'. He has a homely way of expressing his ideal'. "Great heroes of history are nothing to me......I do not want to be a great leader. I want to be a man who goes round with an oil-can and, when he sees a break-down, offers his help. To me the man who does that is greater than any holy man in saffron-coloured robes. The mechanic with the oil-can, that is my ideal in life."

The Tata Institute of Social Sciences showed a fine sense of spiritual discernment when they called their book on Baba Amte and his work: *A Journey from Sympathy to Empathy.*

10

I am a Hindu Brahmin But I am Also a Follower of Jesus Christ

When Baba Amte professes to be a Hindu Brahmin and also a follower of Christ, the question arises: what does he mean by being a follower of Christ? We can safely say that his resolve to be a follower of Christ is not the outcome of a scholarly study of the Christian religion; it rather is the outcome of an intuition. Amte sees in Jesus Christ the perfect expression of the ideal of creative humanism. What attracts Amte are the human values contained in Christ's life and teaching. He sees in following Christ the best way of becoming fully human and fully alive.

Amte did part of his High School studies in a Mission School in Nagpur. The obligatory Bible lessons bored him, but he did come to know the life of Christ. As time went on he could not fail to see that in the way of life he had chosen he actually did follow in the foot-steps of Christ. At a time when people affected with leprosy were expelled from their families and from society and no one dared to come near them, Jesus Christ had a heart for them; he touched them and healed them. Amte could never look at the wounds of leprosy patients without remembering Jesus Christ. He says: "When I come across a leprosy patient, foul smelling, ulcerous, I can see the imprint of His kiss on his forehead. That is all I see, just His lips, His Kiss" (*Karunecha Kalam*, p. 26).

There are many other parallels in the life of Amte and the life of Jesus Christ. Amte has renounced his inheritance to become one with the common people. Jesus was born in a stable, as an outcast for whom there was no place in the inn; when Jesus had started his public life he could say: "The foxes have holes, the birds of the air have nests, but I have no home, I have no place where to lay my head."

Christ broke the rules of respectable people and was blamed for eating with outcasts and sinners. When Amte had become one with leprosy patients he was avoided by all respectable people and could say: "I am more isolated than my patients."

Seeing in Christ the perfect expression of his own ideal, Amte decided to put on the mind of Christ as perfectly as he could. He decided to become 'a contemporary Christ'; that is to say, to act in every moment as he thought Christ would act if he had been in his place.

Amte appears to have been fairly successful in being a contemporary Christ. When Mr. Schnellmann of Swiss Aid met Baba Amte for the first time, he said: "The first fully consistent Christian I have met in my life!"

Amte gives a plain description of what he means by the spirit of Christ. He writes: "Whenever a physician removes pain, and eyes afflicted with blindness get a glimpse of the sun, when people lost in remote dark regions find barefoot helpers, when a ray of light shining through the torn thatch of a hut lights up the mystery of the universe, when a mouthful of bread quells the scorching fire of hunger and a touch of mercy transcends all boundaries of nations and religions, when non-violence challenges power and wealth and mercy overcomes the cruelty of the torturer, it is there that I discover the presence of Christ's spirit" (*Karunecha Kalam* p. 26).

Understanding the following of Christ in this sense, Baba Amte saw no contradiction in claiming to be a Hindu Brahmin and also a follower of Christ.

Through his reading of history Baba Amte knew that there is much in the history of the Church which is not in tune with the teaching of Christ. Amte has no liking for Christians who are more interested in church organization than in the service of the poor. He says: "I am a follower of Christ, but not the sort of Christian who says: 'I have an executive meeting at four-thirty' while there is a man dying in the gutter." (*Graham Turner: More than Conquerors,* p. 186).

Amte knows that Jesus prayed that all may be one. Yet the various Christian Churches fought one another, hated one another, even killed and burned members of other Churches as heretics. Baba's basic conviction is: 'A religion which cannot make its members one with one another, can also not make them one with God."

Amte, therefore, is careful to point out that what he stands for is the genuine spirit of Jesus Christ and that he has no liking for people who call themselves Christians but do not live up to the spirit of Christ. He begins his poem 'Karunecha Kalam' by saying: "Whenever Christianity is in conflict with Churchianity I squarely stand on the side of Christianity, because it is on this side that I have seen Jesus, who lends a helping hand to humanity, conquering forts." Amte is not opposed to a Church which is faithful to the spirit of Christ. In fact he sees the assurance for a brighter future in the communion of many people who not only call themselves Christians but are 'Christs'. He writes: "I saw fearless workers digging the earth near the path of Christ thus strengthening his way of life, and I saw on their sun-burned back rivulets of sweat carve a wet cross. I then had the vision of many Christs and the assurance for a brighter future was mightily strengthened." (*Karunecha Kalam* p. 26).

Prominent Christians like Mother Teresa profess to derive their strength and inspiration from the celebration of the Lord's Supper. Unfortunately Baba Amte never lived in Christian surroundings. He never had an opportunity of experiencing the beauty and the dynamism of a community whose bond of union is the celebration of the Lord's Supper.

Baba Amte does not see the reign of the spirit of Christ confined to people who call themselves Christians. He sees the spirit of Christ at work in all religions, in the wisdom of India's Advaita no less than in the gentle shade of the Bodhi tree. He sees the spirit of Christ at work in all good people to whatever religion they may belong. "I recognized in the palms of Gandhiji's hands the wounds caused by the nails of the Cross, and on the breast of Christ the marks of a pistol's bullets."

The way in which the same spirit, the same ideals and aspirations are at work in the hearts, and minds of prominent leaders belonging to various religions was strikingly in evidence when the Dalai Lama paid a visit to Baba Amte at Anandwan on January 26, 1990.

The Dalai Lama had never been to Anandwan before. But wonderfully familiar did he look in the setting of the paradise which Baba Amte and his associates had created out of nothing. And, as the two stood face to face, the mask of formality melted. Warm smiles and firm hand clasps set up the mood of the meeting. Baba Amte lay in his bed since his stiff spine does not allow him to sit. The Dalai Lama sat on the bed's edge, politely refusing the easy chair Baba's wife, Sadhanatai, offered him. Baba Amte declared: "In Anandwan the basic theme is simple: nature can fulfil our needs, not our greed. We work on a simple premise: sufficiency for all before there is superfluity for some. This is our prescription for peace. Compassion is our tool."

The Dalai Lama was deeply touched by Amte's practice of compassion. He said: "Compassion is a mother's tool too. In the womb, and later as well, physical touch is crucial for the child. But more than that, it is her love, extreme compassion that makes the real difference. I am glad you have the right tool."

As Amte went down the memory lane, recalling how Anandwan became a reality, the Dalai Lama took his glasses off, wiped his tears, and said: "Baba your life is so wonderful. So creative. I admire you."

When taking leave from Anandwan the Dalai Lama said: "Words mere words, such as love, compassion, vision, have no meaning when they are uttered, but here you have translated them into action. Let me do something for you."

He declared that he was donating 20,000 US dollars as the first instalment, then, each year, he would give Rs. 50,000 to Anandwan for five years, as further instalments.

And when the moment of parting came, the Dalai Lama was overcome with an emotion of the tenderest kind. He cried, never trying to hide his tears, and said: "Anandwan is the pilot project for the rest of the world. I will come again." (*Sunday Mail*, Feb. 11-17 p. 18-19).

The Cross as the Symbol of the Spirit of Christ

Amte certainly has a great devotion to the Cross of Christ. At the end of the chapter entitled *Karunecha Kalam* (The Voice of Compassion) he thus addresses Jesus Christ crucified:

"The Cross on which you spent your last breath has become to me not a sign that your service has come to an end, I see in it the sum of all that gives value to our life.

"To me it is not a symbol of violence wrought on you. To me it has become the voice of compassion."

It is not easy to give a coherent explanation of the way in which he sees in the Cross 'the sum of all that give value to our life' or the 'Voice of compassion.' The answer to these questions is bound to remain guess work, since Amte himself has not given an explanation.

There are, however, a few points which are obvious. He sees in Cross the symbol of a spirit which is the very opposite of the hard-heartedness with which many members of the rich elite are affected. He accuses them of being afflicted with mental leprosy: "So many people suffer from mental leprosy. The physical signs of leprosy are a hypo-pigmented patch and loss of sensation. Now in the so-called healthy society you can see a lot of injustice and poverty, yet you are not moved. You have lost your sensation, your feeling. The mind is so dull, the heart so unfeeling, thick-skinned like a hippopotamus – that's mental leprosy."

Amte certainly sees in the cross the symbol of a spirit which is the very opposite of such 'mental leprosy.' Amte feels that Christ by willingly accepting all the pain inflicted on him and all the insults that were hurled against him has entered into 'a friendship of pain with suffering humanity.'

The Cross, a Transforming Power

Amte sees in the cross a transforming power which is at work even today. He expresses this by saying that Christ does no longer bear the cross, but a plough in the form of a cross. The plough is the instrument of preparing fields for the harvest. In the cross he sees the power which can change the hearts of men;

it is the power which can transform the love of life into a life of love and thus prepare fields for the fulfilment of dreams of a happy future. After having stated that only a part of the people who call themselves Christian have put on the mind of Christ he says:

"I have seen a saddened Christ walking on a path at the end of that devotion. He was not then carrying a cross on his shoulders, but the heavy burden of a plough in the shape of a cross. Deep peace shone from the eyes of Him who carries the burden of the world, his face dripping with sweat.

"I immediately forsook the antiquated ways of devotion and began to walk in the footsteps of Christ carrying the plough. This creative bearer of burdens who walks in front of me, still continues on his way. I saw fearless workers digging the earth near the path of Christ, thus strengthening His way of life and I saw on their sun-burned back rivulets of sweat carve a wet cross. I then had the vision of many Christs and the assurance for a brighter vision was mightily strengthened."

When Amte says: "I had the vision of many Christs and the assurance for a brighter vision was mightily strengthened" he obviously means to say that he had the vision of many people who not merely were called Christian but were real Christs, in the sense of having put on the mind of Christ, and it is these people who give us the assurance of a brighter future.

Amte sees Christ's suffering continued throughout the centuries in the cruelty of the rich and powerful, who in a mechanized industrial world exploit the weak and powerless, in the people who tortured to death the inmates of Auschwitz, in the cruelty of people who persecuted and burned Jews and heretics throughout the centuries; in the cruelty of all these people Amte sees the cruelty of those people continued who nailed Christ to the cross and Amte sees Christ continuing his suffering in all these sufferers. Amte says: "Jesus, I have seen your continued dying. When people were burned alive for holding on to your teaching, then I saw that it was your body that was still in agony."

The Cross, the Source of the Stream of Life

The healing influence which the Cross of Christ exerts on mankind Amte presents as a stream which gives life to all that is tender, merciful, true and beautiful. This stream, he says, has its origin in the tears which Mary shed when the body of her son, taken from the cross, rested on her lap.

This stream of tears flowing through the centuries is the enlarged inheritance of the priceless tears shed by Mary when the body of her son, taken from the cross, rested on her lap.

It is this flow of tears that endowed with humanness living statues made of flesh and blood.

The whole stream of mercy and peace, of truth and beauty of love and progress has its source in that tenderness.

In all times and countries, in all religions and castes, lofty person have risen from this stream that is brimful of human tenderness and is superior to all that divides man from man. This stream of compassion, allied to the tears shed, raised visions of a brighter future, visions which have become mine, now and in the days to come.

To the impact which Christ Crucified has exerted on mankind Amte gives expression in the following prayer:

Even murderers you constantly met with creative companionship,

You were found in the worship of the faithful,

You raised questions in the minds of those who had lost faith,

You have become the inspiration of artists and the zeal of social workers; you have become bread for the hungry and consolation for the ailing, support to the helpless, a bright future for those who were in despair, You have become being for those who were lost in nothingness.

(*Karunecha Kalam,* p. 25-30).

Baba Amte says:

Everyone should attempt to walk in the shadow of Christ's cross. That means that you are in the company of that life which scuttled itself to save others. I haven't the arrogance to say that I can carry the mighty load of His cross, but I do try to walk in its shadow (Graham Turner *More than Conquerors,* p. 187).

Christ, the Driving Power in Amte's Life

Mahatma Gandhi did a tremendous service to Christians by showing that the Sermon on the Mount can be put into practice even in public life. Many Christian interpreters had regarded the Sermon on the Mount as a noble ideal that was of little practical importance. Mahatma Gandhi looked on Jesus Christ as the Prince of all Satyagrahis and based his struggle for the independence of India on the Sermon on the Mount. With awe and amazement Christians saw Christ's doctrine put into action in a way they have never thought possible.

Though Gandhiji had such a deep insight into Christ's teaching he never seemed to have come into contact with the person of Christ. Stanley Jones who had done so much to explain Gandhi's teaching to the people of the USA, one day wrote to Gandhiji. "May I suggest that you penetrate through the principles to the person of Christ and then come back to tell what you have found."

The Mahatma wrote back an immediate reply: "I appreciate the love underlying the letter, but my difficulty is of long standing. Other friends have pointed it out to me before now. I cannot grasp the position by the intellect; the heart must be touched. Saul became Paul not by an intellectual effort, but by something touching his heart."

Thus Gandhiji professed that he never had an experience of Christ's presence which would have touched his heart.

The case is different with Baba Amte. He not only saw in Jesus Christ the perfect ideal of creative humanism, he also experienced Jesus Christ as a living presence and as a power which carried him to greater heights and urged him to go on with his work.

In the chapter entitled: तृप्त जखमांचे समृद्ध संस्कार (See Page 108) (Sacred signs of healed wounds imprinted on my heart) Amte compares Jesus Christ to an eagle holding his young one with the claws, carrying it up to sunny heights and protecting it with his mighty wings against wind and storm. Amte acknowledges Christ as the power to lift his life to heights of which he never would have even dreamt of.

"Jesus brought order into my vagrant life and raised me

to heights I would never have dreamt of. The way along which I wandered in a reckless manner following footprints which were marked with fresh red blood, this is the very way along which Christ has travelled, dripping with blood and carrying a heavy cross on his shoulders. Joining work to words to his transforming plough Christ has prepared fields for the fulfilment of dreams of a happy future recklessly spending his flesh and blood as fertilizers.

"He does not run after the joys of life, but life of its own accord has turned to him. Taking pity on the puzzled look on my face he shed light on the path that leads to a glorious future. He urged me to set out on my journey. His constant call was 'Get on with your work.' He gave me light and daring to accept reckless challenges which often were surrounded by mystery and darkness. The vision of His suffering turned out to be the sacred signs of healed wounds imprinted on my heart.

"I only hoped for some rays, but the sun itself rose in my courtyard, giving knowledge of the past, alertness of the present and discriminating acceptance of the days to come. He dragged into freedom that timid ego of mine which kept clinging to the prison bars of today.

"All the springs of true life have their origin with the King of Bethlehem who discerned the desire for true love and holiness even in the hearts of sinful women and respected the dignity of mothers who in their children bear the burden of sin of unknown fathers."

(*Karunecha Kalam* p. 48-51).

After Baba Amte had met many people, who inspired by Christ, take care of the suffering, the oppressed, the fallen, the abandoned and the uneducated, he got the impression that Christ's life did not come to an end when they nailed Him to the cross, that He has risen, indeed, and even today carried on a work of love all over the world. He felt that people who walk in the footsteps of Christ, are moved by the spirit of Christ. Christ became manifest to him as an inspiration, as a mighty creative force which is at work even today. Thus the conviction grew in him that he was doing Christ's work, that Christ is using him as an instrument in continuing His work on earth. In a letter addressed to me, dated 24.8.1985, Baba Amte wrote "In my life He performs the cause which is in my mind and heart."

It is Baba Amte's specific achievement that by relentlessly pursuing his ideal of creative humanism he entered into the world of joy; he succeeded in becoming fully human and fully alive.

He has said: "For me there is no better religion than the one that builds inside the human being a sense of dignity and self-esteem."

By fostering that sense of dignity and self-esteem in the leprosy patients at Anandwan he succeeded in creating that admirable community which is Anandwan. By fostering in people all over India such a sense of dignity and self-esteem he endeavours to co-operate in the building of a New India.

All thoughtful people strive for a deeper knowledge of self and of God. Baba Amte points out that the key to such deeper knowledge is creative humanism, the selfless service of our fellow-men.

On the wall of the hospital at Anandwan the following words are inscribed:

I sought my soul, but my soul I failed to see.
I sought my God, but my God eluded me.
I sought my brother, and I found all the three.

Appendix

MAHAROGI SEWA SAMITI, WARORA *
(Leprosy Service Society)

In accordance with the nominating guidelines, the following information has been compiled in order to clarify the work, achievements and inspiration behind this humanitarian institution.

1. Extraordinary Contributions towards alleviating human suffering:

The inspiration behind ***"Maharogi Sewa Samiti, Warora"*** - 'Leprosy Service Society' is a man who to date has set world standards for the successful rehabilitation of leprosy patients and co-ordinated some of India's most daring and prominent ecological and social programmes.

For centuries society shunned those who contracted leprosy (a deforming disease of the nervous system). The infected could stigmatise their entire family so even close relations abandoned them. Over the last 50 years the people of India have changed their view of leprosy, a change in part attributed to Maharogi Sewa Samiti and its founder **BABA AMTE,** who today is probably the most respected secular figure in the country.

The turning point in Baba Amte's life came one night when in a tropical storm he encountered an abandoned leprosy victim lying in the gutter in the last stages of the disease. The sight of the dying man (Tulsiram Yadav) crawling with maggots, frightened Amte into running away. Ashamed with himself and disgusted by his own weakness he returned to take care of the man until he died.

---

* Abbreviation used in the text hereafter - MSS.

It became apparent to Baba that, ***"WHERE THERE IS FEAR THERE IS NO LOVE, WHERE THERE IS NO LOVE THERE IS NO GOD".*** In a quest to conquer his own fear and that of the society, he decided along with his wife, Sadhana Tai, to dedicate the rest of his life to fighting the problems of leprosy and rehabilitating its sufferers.

He read widely, took a course in leprosy treatment at the Calcutta School of Tropical medicine, attended many seminars and obtained practical experience by working in a leprosy colony. He was convinced that **FEAR** of leprosy was far worse than the disease itself and that such fear must be removed if any meaningful rehabilitation was to be achieved.

He believed that leprosy patients had to be taught skills, to be self-supporting through creative work so that the mental depression derived from the sense of being useless and unwanted can be totally removed. What the patients needed more than anything else was, ***HOPE, DIGNITY AND SELF-RESPECT.*** Baba believed that only work could build a whole human being and so followed the concept - ***"CHARITY DESTROYS; WORK BUILDS."***

MSS was founded on these convictions in 1949, and with invincible optimism, he created **ANANDWAN** - (Forest of Joy) in 1951, thus leaving behind his previous life of a lucrative law practice and an inheritance from a well-off Brahmin family. Along with his wife and two infant sons, Vikas and Prakash, and a handful of patients, Baba Amte moved to 20 hectares of arid rocky land donated by the government. Baba worked and the patients worked shoulder to shoulder with him. It is this quality which distinguishes Anandwan from many other institutions, which only care for the patients' physical needs, but do not try to make them self-reliant individuals, encouraging and training them in some productive work useful to society.

Once started there was no looking back and since those days of hard labour and persistence under difficult conditions, Anandwan has not only served the leprosy afflicted, but extended its humanitarian activities to the other most deprived sections of society. In the following years, orthopaedically handicapped, visually impaired, hearing and speech impaired, young school drop-outs and the abandoned were also brought under the purview of the institution's mission.

Today in Anandwan there are 4000 disabled and disadvantaged people housed in different sites of the institution all engaged in 49 diverse and productive trades and disciplines such as : *AGRICULTURE, INDUSTRIAL PRODUCTION, TEXTILES, PRINTINGS, HANDICRAFTS, LEATHERCRAFTS, WORKSHOP etc.*

Anandwan has become only one of 5 important project sites spread across 300 km of some of Central India's most backward regions. Others include: **ASHOKWAN** (Est. 1957), **SOMNATH** (Est. 1967), **NAGEPALLI** (Est. 1973) and **HEMALKASA** (Est. 1973).

Somnath (Est. 1967) is another major rehabilitation project of the MSS set in the tribal belt of Chandrapur district of Maharashtra, 50 km from the district headquarters. After reclaiming 700 acres of the 1300 acres land allotted by the Govt. of Maharastra, the Samiti has recently launched a micro-watershed project aimed at developing and conserving the land, water and vegetation resources to serve as a base for sustaining five profitable production sectors viz. Food crops, horticulture, fisheries, forestry and animal husbandry.

HEMALKASA, another major success of MSS is set amongst thick forests in the Tribal Belt of Maharashtra. Here the **Madia Gond** tribals have been provided with free medical treatment which benefits 40,000 tribal patients yearly, who come from 1000 surrounding hamlets and villages extending up to a radius of 150 km. Besides this, a residential school caters for 464 children who are given free food, hostel accommodation, education and medical facilities.

The project is run by Baba Amte's son and daughter-in-law, Dr. Prakash and Dr. (Mrs.) Mandakini Amte, who work under difficult conditions to alleviate the suffering and exploitation of these elusive people. In recognition of their benevolent activities, the Royalty of Monaco released a postal stamp giving international acclaim to the Samiti's work.

Under the guidance of the Amte family, MSS has achieved phenomenal results in alleviating human suffering. How these results were achieved can be seen further on in this paper.

The Samiti's aims have always been clear and for sighted, the prime objective being:

1. Medical treatment of leprosy afflicted and other disabled persons.
2. Training and rehabilitation of the physically disabled and socially deprived and disadvantaged persons, through productive work and activities.
3. Educational Development.
4. With Baba's firm belief that the 'Youth' of the country represent a generating force, vocational training given to the socially deprived school drop-outs of rural areas helps them to rehabilitate themselves on return to the villages.

2. An Established record of achievement:

In all its objectives, MSS has achieved success beyond similar areas of work undertaken by many other organisations. This is fair to say and whilst others have fallen by the wayside, the Samiti's work is still going strong.

An estimated 25,000 leprosy patients have been treated and 19,000 rehabilitated since inception. The blind, deaf-mute, handicapped and orphaned have found succour through education and work motivated activities. The rural school drop-outs have found employment through vocational training programmes thus preventing them from turning to crime as on alternative. In addition conservation of the environment, preservation of India's tribal culture and unification of her people have contributed greatly to the improvement of the country. The results of all the institutions' programmes executed over the last 50 years are clear to see and if one considers the list of Honours and Awards (Encl. 1), both national and international, they are as much an established record of achievement as any statistical account of how many have been cured, rehabilitated and inspired over the last half century.

Whilst the figures are astronomical, here is a sample from the recorded statistics of those who have benefited from MSS's work:

A) MEDICAL SERVICES:

1. For medical treatment of leprosy patients the main hospital is at Anandwan. The total number of leprosy patients treated in 3 years (1996-99) is: **4537**
2. Patients under MDT (Multi Drug Treatment): **266**
3. Working population of cured leprosy patients: **967**
4. Old age population of cured leprosy patients staying at **"Snehsawali"** (Old age home for those above 60): **516**
5. The other main centre of medical service is at the Hemalkasa Project where an average 40,000 tribals get medical treatment and other benefits, every year.

B) EDUCATIONAL DEVELOPMENT:

Colleges: The Degree colleges with faculties in Arts, Science, Commerce and Agriculture built by the cured leprosy patients at Anandwan operate under the banner of **'Anand Niketan College'.** The management of these colleges is done by the MSS. The colleges constructed cater to about 2500 non-disabled students of the society from as far afield as Andhra Pradesh and Kerala.

Schools:

1. The two residential schools at Anandwan also similarly constructed are for the visually impaired and the other for the hearing and speech impaired poor children from the rural areas. These cater for a total number of 350 students.
2. At the Hemalkasa project, education of tribal children is conducted by the **"Tribal Ashram School",** started 24 years ago. Today 464 tribal students are given education up to Standard X. The average percentage of students who pass is 70%. Two tribal students from this school have become doctors (M.D.) and are working for the tribals.

C) TRAINING AND REHABILITATION OF PHYSICALLY DISABLED AND SOCIALLY DEPRIVED PERSONS:

i) "Sandhi Niketan" (Est. 1972) - with aid from Take Heart

Foundation (U.K.) - It trains the handicapped (non-leprosy afflicted), like polio-affected, deaf-mute, blind etc. The training is conducted in conjunction with vocational training for a period of 2 years thereafter allowing the students to return to their villages to earn their livelihood. The number of disabled trainees is:
1996-97: total 99 (boys - 71, girls – 28)
1997-98: total 103 (boys - 73, girls - 30)

ii) **"Yuvagram"-Youth Village Programme:** Vocational training for the socially deprived school drop-outs was started 2 years ago at Anandwan and Somnath centres. The youths are given 6 months training (vocational training) after which they can return to their villages in a stronger position to secure employment. Each group is about 50-60 students who in addition to training receive free food, accommodation, medical treatment and a stipend of Rs. 100 each per month.

iii) **"Gokul"** - Caters for about 60 children who are either orphans or children of leprosy patients. Here the children receive food, accommodation, clothing, books, stationary, medical services, transport facilities to school etc.

iv) **"Uttarayan"** - This home for senior citizens caters to around 30 persons, again providing free food, accommodation etc.

D) Productive Activities for generation of revenue and rehabilitation of disabled persons:

Whatever MSS undertakes, it's done with a high degree of quality or it isn't done at all! Concerning agriculture, the projects concerned, produce a higher yield of crops with better quality in comparison to what local farmers produce. The dairy and cattle breeding has resulted in significantly healthy animals. This is in part due to the unique experimental approach to all activities.

The major centre of food production is at Somnath followed by the Anandwan project site. The agricultural activities at Somnath supply the food requirements of all the institutions/projects and are a valuable source of revenue. It's hard to imagine that on land which produces prolific quantities of food and boasts a yield per acre five times greater than the average in the State of Maharashtra was once dead and barren. Wheat, paddy and hybrid corn/sorghum are the three major food grains produced. Different varieties of fruits are also grown at Somnath and Anandwan including lime, coconut, banana, orange, guava, sweet lime, grapes, water melon and custard apple.

3. Innovation in Programme Design:

MSS approach to all its issues of concern has from the onset been characterised by a clarity and uniqueness from the conception of on idea, to its implementation. This can only be attributed to Baba and the rest of the Amte family along with the dedication of their workers.

Whilst other institutions gave **physical** relief to the leprosy afflicted, MSS transformed the lives of thousands of leprosy patients by making them self-reliant and valuable contributors to society.

But the story doesn't end here —under this institution many other activities have been leading the way in improving the quality of life for the most neglected individuals in society as well as pricking the conscience of the society as a whole.

Environmental issues have always been a major concern of the Samiti and the development of many programmes in this field has greatly contributed to environmental awareness. The following are a selection of the most noteworthy of these programmes:

In 1984 the **Agro Forestry Project** was started and is presently one of the most successful projects of its kind in the country. Twenty four forest species were grown in an arboretum for demonstration purposes. A separate forest grove over 2 acres was also established.

Under their **Environmental Awareness Movement** MSS has taken special initiatives in disseminating the result of its research programmes amongst the people of the surrounding regions. The institutions Agricultural faculty has motivated students to take active interest in plantation programmes, the result of which is a **Forest-cum-Garden** of 25,000 trees on the eroded land of the college grounds.

Education and public awareness in the maintenance of environmental balance was organised through a series of activities initiated under the **Vriksha-Ganga** movement. This later progressed towards the famous Knit-India cycle marches by a group of youth lead by Baba Amte throughout the length and breadth of the country. The first march from south to north was organised in 1985-86 from Kanyakumari to Kashmir, and the second from west to east during 1988-89 from Itanagar to Okha. Both had the main objective of promoting national integration and environmental awareness by uniting the people of India, creating inter-state amity, and mobilising the vast potential of **Youth Power.** The importance of protection and preservation of the environment was explained to the people all along the route of these cycle marches. Baba Amte cautioned the people and the administration about the imminent threats posed by the alarming rate of deforestation, and called for action in helping to prevent an environmental and ecological disaster.

More recently the Samiti has taken a leading role in fighting the Indian government's plan for construction of big dams. The dams of the Narmada Valley threaten to create on ecological catastrophe, drown a rich agricultural region, force hundreds of thousands of subsistence farmers off their land and submerge dense forests in which thousands of tribal people live. In July 1988, 80 eminent environmentalists and activists assembled at Anandwan to assert their collective will against the construction of Big Dams in India. The 3 days conference succeeded in forming a common prospective towards the problem. A common document called the **Anandwan Declaration** was unanimously adopted. In addition to this an internationally televised protest of 30,000 people at the village of Harsud was organised further highlighting the urgency of the issue.

The Scientific Management of Water Resources is another initiative undertaken by MSS. At Somnath, Anandwan and other project sites of the Samiti, scientific techniques are being applied for the conservation of water. The approach comprises of building a series of bunds on the small streams to arrest the free flow of rain water during monsoons. Several storage tanks/ponds are constructed to hold rain water. These ponds help to augment the underground water resources thereby raising the level of the water table of the area. Tube wells are constructed near these ponds for supply of irrigation/ drinking water during summer months. The prevention of the free-flow of rain water helps also to control soil erosion. The waste water of all the Anandwan communities is recycled into ponds through drainage canals. Fish are bred in the ponds and feed on the waste food particles, the silt from the bottom is utilised as manure on the surrounding agricultural land.

Low-cost housing technology for rural areas adapted by MSS has gained a wide recognition and is one of the unique activities undertaken by the institution. Based on the Egyptian prototype of **Nubion Arch Cottages** this ancient method of construction has been utilised in all the project sites. The buildings are low in cost and ecologically ideal since they don't require extensive use of timber or cement. In addition to this they have a lower heat capacity in summer and retain heat during the winter. The bricks used in construction are handmade by the institutions workers and are made using only 5% admixture of cement and local mud and sand. Recently a new technique was adopted incorporating crushed plastic waste materials as a method of recycling the otherwise hazardous waste plastics which threaten the environment. An innovation of a new method of low-cost brick laying for the construction of the roof is presently under trial.

There is no requirement of firing the bricks thereby saving fuel and the smaller dimensions of each brick have proved more effective in the building construction by the disabled. The demonstration of ***low external input technology*** in building houses was successfully demonstrated at Killari and Latur in the earthquake affected region of Central India in 1993. The culmination of this demonstration resulted in the Govt. of India concern HUDCO (Housing and Urban Development Corporation), starting a building centre at Anandwan, the only one of its kind in this region.

MSS ensures that nothing is wasted and as such has incorporated non-conventional sources of energy of which their bio-gas plants are one example. A bio-gas plant (Chinese style) measuring 45 m3 has been recently connected to 24 toilets from which the resulting collected methane gas provides a means of cost free fuel for lighting and cooking.

The Samiti's **Tribal Welfare Programmes** as described earlier have gained international recognition for their preservation of the culture of tribals of India who are facing extinction through modern development, exploitation and disease. **Hemalkasa Lok Biradari Project** (The People's Brotherhood) [Est. - 1973) situated in the Gadchiroli district of Maharashtra serves the **Madia-Gond** tribals who are alienated from the outside world. In this particular project primary health care was given top priority. The centre started in 1973 has recently developed into a full fledged hospital having 40 beds which caters for over 40,000 patients annually. Six sub centres were started in the interior forest area, geographically wide apart from the main hospital, of which three are still functional.

A residential school was started in 1976 for the tribal children now giving free education to 464 students. The children receive education in their own crafts and also get an opportunity to earn while they learn.

Other programmes are: practical training in farming, seed production and distribution, dairy, goat and pig farming, health education etc. These programmes are aimed at the survival of the tribals and all efforts have been made to bring about awareness of social rights and duties through continued dialogue and social exposure.

A small sheltered enclosure has been formed at Hemalkasa to keep orphaned babies of wild animals, thereby protecting them from merciless killing. This rescue-cum-orphanage, houses the largest one man collection of wild animals in the country.

Dr. Prakash and Dr. (Mrs.) Mandakini Amte have both worked tirelessly under extremely difficult conditions to help in the preservation of India's tribal people.

The Samiti's founder Baba Amte always believed in the **Creative abilities of the Youth** and thus tried to include them in many of the institution's activities. In the **Bal Taru Palkhi** (a sapling on a palanquin) marches, youths enthusiastically participated in promoting environmental awareness.

To achieve a sustainable agricultural production at a high level the MSS has recently intensified its efforts to develop a watershed project at Somnath. It aims at initiating and implementing programmes to optimise the resource potential of the watershed by adopting technologies related to crop production, horticulture, inland fisheries, agro-forestry and animal husbandry. It is also proposed to study the socio-economic aspects of development with reference to participation of residents and the assessment of benefit.

It is also at the Somnath Project that an annual week-long Youth Camp is held during May every year since 1967 attracting hundreds of high school/college participants from all over India. They participate in physical work and many social, cultural and educational activities.

Finally **The Youth Village Programme** which has been mentioned earlier is a new addition to the Anandwan/Somnath projects. Providing for approximately 60 students (school drop-outs from the rural areas), it gives 6 months vocational training in a number of skills (Metal work, Printing, Sewing, Industrial production, maintenance of diesel engines, welding etc.) enabling them to return to their villages and find local employment. Without harnessing the potential of these young individuals many might have taken to crime as a means of financial support. In Anandwan they learn the values of the **Community Spirit** by the example of the other inmates. It is interesting to note that whilst previously the local members of the town society had shunned those affected by leprosy, they now find help, encouragement and training from the institutions constructed by the cured patients, an indication of the Samiti's success in Leprosy rehabilitation.

4. Organisational Capacity and Administrative Efficiency:

It's incredible when one considers that MSS was started with only 20 hectares of arid waste land donated by the government, a handful of leprosy patients, a lame cow and Rs. 14/-. Its success is attributed only to the clear sightedness and impeccable business like implementation of all its projects by Baba Amte and his sons.

At the apex level, MSS is now managed by a committee of trustees consisting of 15 members. The control, guidance and management of the Samiti's affairs are carried out by the governing body whose members are elected every 3 years. The office bearers of the Samiti are elected from amongst the members of the Samiti. Any vacancy occurring is filled by the governing body during the next election. The governing body takes decisions about the investment and utilisation of the Samiti's funds and all deeds and documents on behalf of MSS are executed by the governing body.

Not a penny is wasted, the accounts are subjected to a number of checks in order to protect against careless losses and embezzlement. The non-bureaucratic self-governing culture here sees to it that only very small part goes to salaries. With economic ingenuity and implements, structures are built with multi purposes in mind. And considering that human resources are India's big strength, it isn't surprising that the MSS carefully allocates people's power for peak efficiency.

Most of the people working in different capacities are either cured patients, rehabilitated handicapped persons, or patients who are still undergoing treatment but can still contribute to the economic activity. It is therefore extremely difficult to draw a defining line between employees and beneficiaries. You can thus find at Anandwan post office, a post master who is a cured leprosy patient, teachers in schools who are also cured leprosy patients, or physically handicapped, and numerous technicians, electricians, workmen, artists, gardeners, dairy workers, cooks, compounders, nurses, clerks, attendants etc. who are either completely cured or are fit enough to undertake an activity of their choice and contribute whatever they can. The model being practised at MSS believes strongly in giving patients ***"A CHANCE NOT CHARITY"***, an opportunity to work with dignity and a sense of purpose. Except for a few doctors and retired professionals, the Samiti has hardly any professionals either in management, accountancy, architecture, an engineering and agriculture etc. —the expertise in these areas is home grown!

5. Demonstration of long-term impact:

The MSS has travelled a long way. Starting with a concern for individual development through treatment, rehabilitation and active inducement of leprosy patients in communes shunned by the rest of the community, the Samiti moved on to the assimilation of the handicapped in the same communes. Development of appropriate tools and technology to provide work to all members irrespective of their handicap, and treatment, education and training of Tribals in remote areas formed the next phase of its activities. Soon the success of its economic endeavours was so pronounced that this institution started contributing to the prosperity of the larger society. Finally it has reached the present juncture where, in addition to its earlier objectives, topical social concerns like protection of the environment, awakening of the youth and integrated rural development, have become its pro-occupations.

This journey from the development of the individual to community development and area development has been a long journey, signifying the triumph of the human spirit and effort and 50 years on the results are clear to see. The example Anandwan has been setting in treatment and rehabilitation of leprosy patients has in part altered society's view of this previously unacceptable disease. Through its tremendous work it has taught us to accept, relate to and treat leprosy patients like other normal human beings and ever to encourage them to contribute as others do. It is fair to say that the long term impact of this ideology set by Anandwan has contributed greatly to the overall acceptability of leprosy in India as a curable disease.

The adoption of other societal development concerns by MSS reflected eloquently in its ongoing projects shows that the institution is moving with the times and is always trying to respond to contemporary crises and problems.

The results cannot be measured in precise terms, but it is a fact that MSS under the guidance of Baba and the rest of the Amte family, has quite simply changed the lives of millions. Whether they are leprosy patients, orthopaedically handicapped, blind, deaf-mute, orphaned, and tribal or youth drop-outs, every excluded or undervalued member of society has been included in the Samiti's activities and projected to a level of self-confidence and self-sufficiency regardless of the disability or disadvantage. That is no mean feat. It is quite simply amazing and with Baba currently residing on the banks of the Narmada, the fight to eradicate injustice and exploitation goes on.

"I sought my Soul,
My Soul I could not see,
I sought my God,
My God eluded me,
I sought my brother,
And I found all three"

(words inscribed at Anandwan)

MAHAROGI SEWA SAMITI, WARORA
At & Post: ANANDWAN,
Via:Warora, 442 914,
Dist. Chandrapur,
Maharashtra State, India.
Phone. No. 00 91 7176 82034 / 82425,
FAX No. - 82134.

Bibliography

Publications by Baba Amte:

Jwala ani Phule, Sadhana Prakashan, Pune, 1964
Workers University (in Marathi and Hindi) Sadhana Prakashan, Pune, 1965.
Sarvajanik Sansthanche Sanchalan, Sadhana Prakashan, Pune, 1965
Ujjwal Udyasathi, Sadhana Prakashan, Pune, 1973
Karunecha Kalam, Vasudha Prakashan, Nagpur, 1984
Cry, Beloved Narmada, Anandwan, 1989.

Works about Baba Amte:

Grace Mathew, (Project Director): *A Report on the Project for Documentation of Baba Amte's work,* Tata Institute of Social Sciences,
Bombay.
A cyclostyled copy of this Report was kindly put at my disposal.
This Report is now published in book form under the title: *'A Journey from Sympathy to Empathy - Baba Amte and His Work',* Tata Institute of Social Sciences, Bombay, 1990.
UNICEF: *An Unbeaten Track, A Report on Anandwan.* An experience in community development. UNICEF, New Delhi, December, 1983.
We quote it: UNICEF Report.
Malati Deshpande: *Baba Amte and the Jungle of Happiness,* Sane Guruji Kathamala, Bombay (Date not given).

Books containing chapters on Baba Amte:

Robert A. de. J. Hart: *Ecosociety,* Chapter 13: Design for a World. Natraj Publishers, Dehra Dun.

G. Turner: *More than Conquerors,* Chapter 10, pp. 167-189. Hodder and Stoughton, London, 1976

Arthur Tarnowski, *The Unbeaten Track,* Chapter 16: Anandwan, Amte's Miracle, Chapter 17: Sandhi-Niketan, the End of the Track. Numerous articles in periodicals and daily papers. A long list of the more important articles can be found in the above mentioned work on Baba Amte, published by the Tata Institute of Social Sciences.